THE PYTHON TRAIL

THE PYTHON TRAIL

An Immigrant's Path from Cameroon to America

Richard Afuma, with Thatcher Freund

Down East Books

Camden, Maine

Published by Down East Books
A wholly owned subsidiary of The Rowman & Littlefield Publishing
Group, Inc.
4501 Forbes Boulevard, Suite 200, Lanham, Maryland 20706
www.rowman.com

Unit A, Whitacre Mews, 26-34 Stannary Street, London SE11 4AB

Distributed by National Book Network
Copyright © 2015 by Rowman Littlefield

British Library Cataloguing in Publication Information Available

Library of Congress Cataloging-in-Publication Data

Afuma, Richard.
The python trail: An immigrant's path from Cameroon to America / by Richard Afuma,
with Thatcher Freund.
p. cm.
ISBN 978-1-60893-405-8 (pbk. : alk. paper) -- ISBN 978-1-60893-407-2 (electronic)

∞™ The paper used in this publication meets the minimum requirements of American National Standard for Information Sciences Perma-
nence of Paper for Printed Library Materials, ANSI/NISO Z39.48-1992.

Printed in the United States of America

To my beloved mother, Theresia Kouh-Fien, for her enduring love, care, and inspiration. I feel extraordinarily fortunate that as I write this dedication in August 2013, my mother is still alive at the age of 78, having exceeded by more than forty years her life expectancy at birth. And also to my cheerful and precocious daughter, Alexis Kouh-Fien Afuma.

INTRODUCTION

Americans know that many people in the world want to live in the United States and they know in a vague way that illegal immigrants face great hardships to get here. What strikes me, though, as an immigrant, is that Americans do not appreciate how lucky they are to live here. Where prosperity is normal, one doesn't much reflect on it. Where sex scandals and abuses of power and the gridlock in Congress are front-page news, one loses sight of how much better the government is here than it is most other places in the world.

More than anything, Americans cannot know the depths of envy that most people in the world have for those who live in this country, or the intensity of the desperation for a better life that leads people to give up their life savings in order to cross a desert at night in the faint hope that they will not be quickly caught and deported, or, if they are not deported, that they will find a job picking cotton or apples or asparagus from dawn to dusk and a trailer to share with nine or ten other hopeful souls.

I was born in a mountainous region of Cameroon, a country many Americans cannot place on a map. Cameroon lies in West Africa, east of Nigeria. It possesses three hundred miles of coastline on the Atlantic Ocean. It was once a colony of Germany; later, of France and Britain. Its official languages are French and English, but some two hundred other tongues are spoken there. It is neither the richest nor the poorest nation on the continent. It exports timber, coffee, bananas, tea, cocoa, palm oil, tobacco, sugar, cotton, rice—and people, I should add, like me.

More specifically, I come from a region of the country called Kom, a beautiful land of mountains and savannahs that is home to the tribe from which I derive my identity. We have our own language, one of the two hundred in the country, and our own customs, traditions, history, and legends. My mother, my brother, my sisters, aunts, and uncles still live there. Indeed, I feel much more a Kom than I do a Cameroonian.

But though I come from a specific place, and though at home I'm something of a celebrated figure, in the United States I am just another immigrant. My story—of the twisting path, the hardships, the nearly insurmountable obstacles I overcame to find my way from a primitive village in Africa to the United States—is hardly new. Millions, literally—some twelve million in the last forty years alone—have faced the same sorts of hardships, the same sorts of obstacles as I to make their ways here. Thousands have faced beatings, torture, prison in their native lands of a kind that I cannot possibly imagine.

Even so there are many reasons to tell stories like mine. I've often thought of this. I want to tell my story to preserve a record of my family's history for my daughter and her descendants after her. I want to tell the story of my country. As much as anything I want to tell the story of the Kom, in order to introduce them to the world. The central legend of the Kom, and how they came to live in their beautiful green mountains in a far corner of the world, involves a great snake whose twisting path led them there. It's a good metaphor to describe the journey that I made, and a good metaphor too for every other immigrant, who should know that twisting paths and perseverance can lead them here, and that America, however flawed, is a destination that's well worth the effort.

CHAPTER ONE

During the bright cool mornings of the dry season my friends and I hunted grasshoppers on Fungom Hill. Though they appeared to cover every surface of the grasses waving in the fields and to hang in clumps like bats from the branches of the trees, one worked in a frenzy for an hour just to fill a soda bottle with the things. The rocks on those mornings were cold and disagreeable to our bare feet, but morning was the only time to catch these creatures. The presence of the dew beading on green leaves seemed to slow their escapes. The effort, though exhausting, was so exhilarating that even in our zeal we found time to squeal with laughter. The little children not yet skilled enough to catch the grasshoppers danced around us, pointing this way and that to yet another likely prey.

When we had filled our bottles we carried the grasshoppers home to our mothers, who fried them in palm oil with salt and hot peppers, or boiled them skewered ten to twenty on a stick. We savored them. Indeed, hunting grasshoppers was an activity of such significance that we brought our first catches of the year to honored friends and relatives, who gave us prizes for our gifts to them. It was something like Christmas in Fungom then, everyone taking great pleasure in the exchanging of their tokens. I have heard of people traveling to distant villages to make a present of the season's first catch, though I never did so myself.

On those nights when we had finished eating them, my mother would smile at me with warm affection.

"You are a great warrior, Ayeah!" she would say. "But now it is time for great warriors to go to bed."

She had named me Ayeah in honor of her father.

The village of Fungom spread from the top of Fungom Hill, where we lived in the compound of my Uncle Samuel Seing Ngaii, down the hill's half-mile slope. From the top we could see, in one direction, the even greater Bobong Hill, and, in the other, in the lovely green Mughom River Valley below, the village of Belo. There was no electricity in Fungom, or running water, and yet these facts were of no consequence to me as I knew nothing of either one. In Fungom in those days the advancements in technology reached from fire, with which we cooked, through the Iron Age, which gave us pots and pans, and, finally, at the apex of human development, to the hand-turned corn grinder that stood in the compound of the Fungom Village Head.

It is true that kerosene had made its way in Fanta and Coca-Cola bottles to our village. Though I could never have conceived of the sweet fizzy liquid that had once filled these bottles, I did not think that either the kerosene or the lantern flames for which it was essential were anything like magic. They merely existed, like the baskets that my mother wove and the scythes that cut the grass and the mud bricks that men formed to build our houses with. It is also true that on occasion strange things beyond my comprehension crossed the sky above our village. They were said to be "aeroplanes" and to carry people inside. In my imagination these things were enormous, noisy birds, but how or where the people might be carried in their bellies I could scarcely imagine.

I understood from an early age that two peoples inhabited the earth—the Kom and the Bamessi; that we, the Kom, were superior in every way to the Bamessi; that we had an impossibly rich and fascinating history; and that this history centered around the tale of a Kom leader's transformation into a python, which I believed absolutely. I believed that the rolling hills, the wooded slopes, and the fertile farmland of our country were gifts from God, and should be viewed from a perspective of utmost pride and satisfaction. I believed that my people possessed a mystical ability to bring from the soil all that it could give and that the noblest of all callings was to farm a piece of one's own land. Later I would learn that the Kom inhabit an area of roughly 300 square miles—that is to say, not more than 30 miles on the longest course that one might take through it—in Cameroon's North-West Region. Then, though, the idea of a land larger than that which I could see from the top of Fungom Hill did not occur to me.

I couldn't read. We had no radios or television. Other than the stories I was told, my world consisted of nothing more than what I saw: houses made of mud bricks with roofs of thatched grass or corrugated tin; children playing in their dusty yards; men dressed in long shirts and baggy trousers and women in embroidered skirts and blouses. The people of Fungom worked or did not work as they might have been inclined: the industrious, the lazy; the rich, the poor; the young, the old; the healthy and infirm. I watched carpenters erecting houses, farmers tending to their coffee plants, and sellers of kola nuts hawking their fruit about the village. The corn rose in the fields; the goats grazed in the pastures; in the compounds that gave the form to Fungom, orange, mango, and avocado trees blossomed and bore fruit. These compounds numbered 25 or so, and ranged in size from small plots to the several spreading acres of the compound owned by our Village Head. Rows of eucalyptus trees formed the boundaries of the compounds, which each possessed a house for the patriarch as well as houses for each of his wives and their children. A man might have one wife or many. The Village Head had six.

My Uncle Seing was a distinguished, dark-skinned man, with a long nose and upper lip, who possessed the kind seriousness of a respected village elder. Uncle Seing had built our house for us and given my mother lands to farm. Of all my relations he was the one who most expressed his love for our family. It was he who most accepted my mother as a member of his own family; he who went out of his way to help us. My mother told me once that she had never once quarreled with the man.

His compound stood at a crossroads of paths that led to the four corners of the world, and was therefore a locus of activity. People passing by stopped to wave and chat, and at my mother's invitation came into our house for a drink of water or a bite to eat. Her generosity was so widely known that men and women alike passed the compound of my uncle pretending further destinations, in order to accept her hospitality.

By any estimation my mother is, even today, a beautiful woman, with a long, narrow face and skin the color of cocoa, and a sharp aristocratic nose. She's quite tiny as I see her now—not much more than five feet tall—though when I was a child she did not seem small to me. Her eyes are deeply hooded by her brow, a feature which today gives her the look of one who has known all the world's cares, but which in her youth gave her an air of mystery. She speaks only my native tongue, Itanghikom, and has never learned to read or write. She smokes a pipe. Indeed, one of the lasting images of my youth is that of my mother bent before the kitchen fire, pipe in mouth, as she stirred some savory stew. To this day I retain a scar that formed from a bit of ash falling on my chest as I nursed at her breast.

I held such an honored place as my mother's eldest son that I believed I was something of a prince. My Uncle Seing was a second cousin rather than an uncle, though the distinction, even had it been described, would have been lost on me. I might have understood that my mother was not the wife of Uncle Seing, and that, alone of the mothers in the village, she had no husband. Regardless, this fact did not matter. I believed every man in Fungom to be my father. I also understood that by some complex calculation I belonged to the family not of my own biological father, but of my mother's first husband, Maiyili. Though this Maiyili was deceased, I was told that he came from an important and powerful family, and that because of my ill-understood relation to the man, I too had powerful connections.

Our house consisted of a single room without a floor. At the center of the room stood my mother's round hearth, where eucalyptus embers heated the cauldron where she cooked and jars of peppers ringed the hearthstones. Balls of boiled cornmeal known as fufu formed the center of our meals. My mother made njama-njama, a green leafy vegetable served with garlic, tomatoes, and peppers, and soups of cassava, yams, and groundnuts. On special occasions she rewarded us with the crisped meat of a blue duiker—a smallish animal, something like an antelope; or bat meat, which I loved. When the meal was ready I carried to Uncle Seing's house his portion of the meal. We ate by the fire, my mother, my sisters, my two younger brothers and I, each in the place assigned to him or her, dipping our fufu corn into our soup, and, afterwards, sipping from a cup of tea.

Until I reached the age of six my chores around the house were light, for my mother did not believe that so great a warrior as I ought to chop firewood or carry water from the well. Besides the grasshoppers that I liked to catch, I picked avocados which she could sell. In the mornings like other boys in our village I led our goats to pasture, and, in the afternoons, I led them home again. Their leads were made of braided grass and often broke. And when, untethered, the goats scampered off, we chased after them, laughing and screaming, until they ran into somebody's house or were otherwise forced into a corner.

I wanted nothing. My world extended no more than five miles, past the Baptist church in Kikfuini and just beyond a large farm in the village of Mejang that was owned by Uncle Seing. I began at the age of six to help my uncle cultivate this farm. The walk took two hours, up rocky hills, down narrow paths in single file, through woods and dense brush that waved back and forth in the sultry breezes. In the rainy season clouds of mosquitoes followed us unceasingly, and we stopped frequently to cover our bodies with palm oil in a vain effort to keep them off. We'd spend several nights at my uncle's farmhouse there, where we learned to grow crops of rice, corn, beans, and cassava.

We planted seeds. We pulled weeds and carried water. We harvested the corn with wicker baskets strapped to our backs, and helped to thresh the rice. The work was long, hot, brutal. Our hands grew calloused, our grips firm, the muscles of our arms sinewy and strong, even at an early age. The baskets of produce that we carried on our heads from the farm to Fungom Village could weigh thirty pounds or more. After two hours on the road our necks grew so stiff from these efforts that it could take a half hour to stretch them out again.

My mother, my uncles, indeed every adult I knew expected such hard work from their children. We accepted it. And yet though we were expected to labor long and hard, there was as well a benefit in it. We were given more responsibility than Western children are and fended much more for ourselves, in consequence of which we were allowed a greater independence than children in developed countries have. When not at work we went anywhere we wished, and so long as we did not cause mischief did anything we pleased.

We walked everywhere—to visit friends and relatives to help them harvesting their crops; to search out firewood; to pick the fruit that hung in such abundance from the trees. On Sunday mornings we walked to the church in Kikfuini. This structure was made of mud bricks no different from those that walled our house, but boasted of a rusty, corrugated metal roof, topped by a white cross. The pastor, himself a Kom, must have preached the gospels, though I have no memory of this. What I recall of religion from my early life are the stories Mother told of God and Moses, of the Good Samaritan, of the life of Christ on earth.

I remember no less vividly than the tale of loaves and fishes the stories Mother told me of the juju. These juju were great hideous creatures, some covered in feathers and some in garish costumes, who wore dreadful, terrifying masks. I had, indeed, a more intimate knowledge of the juju than I had of Jesus Christ, because the juju came out at our village celebrations to dance their terrible dances, when drums were beaten and ankle beads were rattled.

It was puzzling to me at that young age to see that when these specters had finished with their business they were rewarded by the villagers with money or small items of value, and even, occasionally, with a chicken or a goat. But then, at that age one takes for granted that the puzzling things in life are nothing more or less a truth than the truth that one must have food in order to survive.

From the dire warnings of my mother I believed that the juju would snatch me up if I did not behave, and that, in fact, they and other wicked things were waiting for me in the dark, just outside our door at night. My mother's descriptions of these evil beings could not be fantasy: they were confirmed by everyone I knew. The power of sorcery was no less a fact in Fungom than the divinity of Christ.

It is possible that I also connected this sense of magic with the day that a man came from Kikfuini to take what my mother called a "photograph" of us. I had never heard of such a thing and could not imagine what it was, but the importance of the occasion was not lost on me. For weeks we had heard about little else than the impending visit of this man. My mother bought us new clothes, and, the night before, washed and scrubbed us each with care. The photographer was a gruff man, proud of his profession. He lined us up against my uncle's house, over whose wall he had draped a dark sheet—my mother at one end seated in a chair with my baby sister on her lap; my siblings standing in the middle; and I, last in line, dressed in white cotton shorts and a white shirt which Mother had buttoned to the top, serious, standing at attention. This positioning of me as if to anchor the family at the end opposite my mother was an accident, I think. And yet it seems in retrospect entirely appropriate that I should have been placed thus. As the first son of a single woman I was unquestionably the head of our family and master of my siblings' fates.

"Ndzi," "Nyah," "Matimewu," Mother often called me. "Husband," "Father," "Son."

"You are the father of these children," she would say. "These children are your power. People respect you because of them."

My mother revered me, and though she loved her other children, the truth of it, I know, is that she did not esteem them quite as highly. The first boy in any Kom family holds a position of such importance that women weep who have no sons. Such women are believed to be cursed by people who believe in curses, and ridiculed for their deficiency by relations, friends, and mere acquaintances. First sons are groomed for greatness. At meals they take larger portions than their siblings. Though expected to work no less hard than others, their work is more highly praised. If there is money to send a single child to school, the first son always goes.

In these ways I was honored not only by my mother but by my siblings, who in a way also thought of me as their father. Every other relative, everyone I knew to the limits of my world regarded me more highly than they did my brothers and my sisters. No other people, no other culture existed but my own. No one, with the exception of the Village Head, was more important than I; no one but he was respected any more. Thinking now about the status that I held, recalling the fruit that hung in such abundance from our trees and the fresh food that filled our plates and the joy of chasing grasshoppers through the fields, I have come to see that despite the cruel work that was essential to existence, my life was an idyll, and Fungom Village was an Eden.

That is not to say that unhappiness had been banished from the place. What I remember most, other than the trudging back and forth to the farm of Uncle Seing, resulted from diseases that were common—diseases and their preventatives and cures, I should say. Lice crawled so thickly on our heads that our mothers shaved us regularly. Scabies mites ran freely through our clothes and buried themselves in our skin and caused wretched itching. Enormous, vicious fleas called jiggers dug themselves into our feet, and could only be removed by determined mothers at the point of a pin or sharpened stick.

To ward off the malaria that is endemic to those parts, we were forced to swallow quinine pills. Worms were cured with Castor oil.

Nor were Western medicines alone employed. For general preventatives my mother washed us once a year with special grasses that she had soaked in water. She sometimes made us drink the water too.

My mother believed that illnesses were caused by evil magic and believed in the power of traditional healers. People walked six hours and more to visit especially effective sorcerers, though my mother had found some men she liked much closer to home. These medicine men were grave, awe-inspiring personages. I remember their visits vividly: the potions they had brought along in little bottles; the shells of snails which they used for mixing; the ashes, and sometimes, the Castor oil which, when added to the potions, formed a paste. Most clearly I remember the cuts that the medicine men made across my hands and wrists, and the feel of the cool pastes as they were spread across the cuts. My mother paid the men, sometimes with a chicken. The effectiveness of their treatments was proved time and time again in the cures they effected.

So too, from the endless games we children played in and out among the houses of the compounds, did accidents inevitably occur. Once, during a game of hide-and-seek, I gashed my knee on a broken jar that had lain hidden underneath a bed. I was shocked at first, by the sight of so much blood.

My oldest sister was shocked as well.

"*Nawain! Nawain! Nawain! Nawain!*" She screamed across the compound for my mother, who had gone next door to visit.

My mother rushed into our house. My leg was bandaged and, in time, the bleeding stanched.

There were no disinfectants in Fungom, or doctors who might have sewn the wound. Such were the circumstances of our lives that for three weeks, whenever I had to travel any distance in my mother's company—the two miles to Kikfuini, the mile or so to Sho—she was forced to pack me on her back. I cannot say that I have ever much regretted the experience of that painful incident.

The scar I've carried with me ever since recalls those days in such detail that I have often thought the price of that memory rather cheap.

My mother had scarce resources to afford my place in the little school run by Baptist missionaries in the village of Belo, and yet when I was four she began to send me there. This trip is not an easy one, for Belo, though no farther from our house than Kikfuini, lies at the end of a much more difficult trail. The area generally is very rugged. Elevations can rise and fall more than two thousand feet from mountaintop to valley floor. Fungom Village, which is so small and so remote that even Google has not yet found it, lies a little more than 4,000 feet above sea level. The paths that wind up and down the hills are treacherous.

In the dry season this walk takes an hour. In the rainy season it can take much longer. How my mother managed to carry me from Fungom to Belo each weekday morning for the first two weeks of school, and, in the afternoons, back to Fungom again, I cannot say. Thereafter, following a breakfast of fufu corn and cocoyams, I walked by myself in the company of other children.

At the Belo Primary School until the age of six the curriculum and duties were quite informal; discipline was light. Later, the students' lives were much more highly regimented. Uniforms were required of us beyond the age of five—khaki shorts and dark green shirts that were to be well tucked in, or you would get a beating with a eucalyptus branch. You got a beating if your clothes weren't clean. You got a beating if you did not stand up to answer the questions of your teacher. For small infractions one might get a sharp rap or two across each hand. Greater sins deserved greater punishments. I recall that we were once asked to bring to school a bundle of bamboo sticks with which the authorities intended to build a new classroom. I forgot to bring my sticks. I believe that I was caught up in the struggle of a soccer game, but whatever the cause I was beaten on my back and buttocks until they bruised.

I took the beatings for granted. So did everybody else. To we Kom—indeed, to everyone in Cameroon—they were a necessary part of raising children. Discipline is stricter there. Children are required to treat their elders with more respect. In my native country we think that children benefit rather than are harmed by learning the lessons of right and wrong at the end of a eucalyptus branch. It's among the few things in America that I find troubling, in fact, to see children addressing their elders disrespectfully. It's possible that I will change my mind about this, but I don't rule out spanking any child of mine. I believe I'm a better person for being disciplined this way.

The school day began with the ring of a bell, when we met on a soccer field of mud and grass that was bounded on one side by the school, and on the others by stands of guava and eucalyptus trees. There were fifty of us, more or less. We marched in step, the girls in one line, the boys in another, into the school hall for a devotional talk. Older children beat drums and clashed pairs of cymbals, or played tunes on bamboo flutes as we swung our arms in rhythm, singing songs like "Kumbaya" and "Go down, Go down, Go down to Egypt and tell Pharaoh, 'Pharaoh, let my people go!'" We sang "Onward Christian Soldiers," too, although, because I had somehow failed to learn its words, I merely hummed along. The songs inspired me, as they've continued to inspire me all my life. I sing them in church. I sing them to myself, aloud or silently, keeping time in my head and humming "Onward Christian Soldiers" exactly as I hummed it so many years ago. In hard times they give me strength, just as they gave strength before the American Civil War to the slaves working plantations in the South.

When we children had finished singing on our soccer field we marched in single file to class, where our studies would commence. We worked hard all morning. At noon we went outside for lunch to eat what we had brought along. Large midday meals are not usual in Kom. I rarely carried even a snack to school, and found myself each afternoon begging in my most convincing voice for food from my friends. There was a sense even there at school, as there was within my village, that we might depend on the large, extended family for all the things we needed. In Belo as in Fungom people helped their neighbors at planting and harvest times. My mother and her friends ran a sort of credit union called a *njangi*, in which, every month, they met to pay small sums into a kitty for the general good. In our village, at school, elsewhere in our world, everybody shared. I believe that all of us understood that life was a struggle; that, in many ways for most of us, life was a dead end. And so my friends might give me half a kola nut or a piece of their banana, a slice of mango, an orange section.

Each Friday when school was out we sang a song that I can still hear clearly, and which resonates with me as among the most essential things that I have ever done.

"We come to school on Monday, Tuesday and Wednesday, Thursday and Friday is time for us to go," went the song. "Goodbye to you teachers, goodbye to you teachers, goodbye to you teachers is time for us to go."

We sang this song, smiling and waving to our instructors as we made our ways down our separate paths towards home, until they were out of sight. There was something so joyful in its tune and so lovely in its sentiment of respect and gratitude, that whenever I call the song to mind it evokes no less joy in me than it did when I was four.

The memory of those happy days is, I think, among the reasons that I want to tell my story and the story of my people—happy days in a hard world, so far removed from my present one as to seem puzzling. Could I have been beaten with the branch of a eucalyptus tree? Did we catch grasshoppers on Fungom Hill and eat them on a stick? Can a boy of six really have walked for hours down rocky paths with a heavy basket on his head?

My daughter will never know such experiences except from the stories I tell her. She will have felt the cold of winters such as I could never have imagined. She will have learned the joy of swift communication. She will know the speed of cars and the weight-lessness of planes, and she will know as I did not that the ocean is an endless thing. She will fear many things, but without my stories she would never fear the juju. She will fall ill, but she will never itch as I itched or feel the sharp stick digging jiggers from her feet, unless I describe these things to her.

I am an immigrant like any other. I am no one. I was neither a boy soldier nor a victim of terror or oppression. And yet, I know, as much as the boy soldiers have to give the world in the lessons of their lives, they can't evoke the lessons that come of ordinary tales.

One writes one's story for many reasons. I have felt ever since those days in Belo that my fate would, somehow, take me to America. I am a man of my world. I believe in the nobility of the Kom people. I believe in the juju—not literally as evil spirits, perhaps, but for the splendor of their costumes and the wonder they evoke. I believe in God the Father Almighty and the Ascension of His son. I believe in destiny. I believe in the power of my mother's love for me, in the force of her ambition for her oldest son, in the respect I have for her, and in the thanks that I'll forever owe her.

CHAPTER TWO

My mother was born sometime around 1935 and named Kouh Fien. Later, as is common with the Kom, she took a Christian name—Theresia. She was one of more than fifty children fathered by Ayeah Nsom, an affluent farmer in the village of Anjin who had nine wives and possessed ten houses as well as farms and other real estate. His daughter's childhood was by all accounts a happy if unexceptional one. As a great beauty and the offspring of a wealthy man, my mother was able in her early teens to marry a prosperous trader named Maiyili, whose last name, if he had one, has been lost to her memory, and who, himself still in his teens, had already taken two wives. Maiyili owned ten wagons and employed a number of village men to carry kola nuts to Nigeria, and, on the return trip, to bring back ready-made clothes and bolts of cloth, rubber shoes, pots and pans, umbrellas and the like. He was wealthy enough even at such a young age to have sent a young relative of his to university—itself a quite astonishing accomplishment—and so handsome that he had earned the nickname "Fine Boy."

The events surrounding my mother's marriage to Maiyili recall such sad memories that she finds it difficult to discuss that time of her life. She's told me very little about it except to say that their love was deep and passionate, and to describe the circumstances of his death. The story of this season of my mother's life has the vagueness and easy lessons of a rumor that time has elevated into legend. There is doubtless some truth to it. At the very least, elements of this story have always been taken for fact.

Some time before Maiyili married my mother, while he was living with his first wife in the compound of his father, the young man's success was already such that he had bought a horse—the only one in Anjin. It is said that Maiyili's father, a layabout named Chiamusoh who had long been jealous of his son, was driven to a peak of envy by the purchase of this horse. Sometime later—days, perhaps, or weeks, or months—the horse is said to have turned up missing. Perhaps as the story goes it was discovered in the nearby village of Fuli. Perhaps, as the Fuli Village Head is reported to have claimed, Chiamusoh had traded the animal to him for a wife.

In consequence of his father's thievery, Maiyili removed himself from Chiamusoh's compound. In time he took a second wife, and then a third—my mother—who bore him a single child, my oldest half-sister Eunice. My mother looked forward to a long life with her husband, and to bearing him a string of children. She had, indeed, all that a woman at that time in the remotest region of Cameroon could ever hope to have. Only the jealousy of Maiyili's father, which Mother doubtless saw for herself, marred what she would have otherwise considered a perfect marriage.

One cannot imagine that the relationship between father and son had ever been a happy one: the propensity for envy, after all, does not appear suddenly in a man's middle age. Neither does it sound farfetched that Chiamusoh would one day approach Maiyili for a loan, or that Maiyili, knowing his father to be a spendthrift and an unreliable debtor, would refuse. Though there is in this tale of Maiyili and his father a disquieting breeziness and a failure of the sort of hard facts necessary to an honest account, it's possible that the central and most astonishing element of this story is true. Anything is possible.

In fact it is undisputed that Maiyili grew ill one day; that his illness defeated local diagnoses; and that his friends and family lost all hope for his recovery until a cousin, returning to Anjin from working the plantations of the coast, advised that he be carried thirty miles to the hospital in Bamenda. Such a trek could not be undertaken lightly. Plans must be made, the necessary men gathered for the purpose. As it was harvest time, the villagers set off one morning for the fields, leaving Maiyili at home in bed. Returning in the afternoon the villagers are said to have found the door to Maiyili's house barred, and when, at last, they gained entrance to the room, they found Chiamusoh dressed in the outfit of a juju, and my mother's husband lying dead in bed. A raw egg, one of the traditional tokens of the Kom funeral ritual, is said to have been placed inside Maiyili's mouth; his mouth and nose had both been tied shut. He had been murdered, or so it is maintained, by means of strangulation.

My mother and her relatives agree that no consequence was levied on Chiamusoh for this supposed act of filicide, except that he was thereafter shunned by the community.

Following Maiyili's death, the story of my mother's life becomes more credible even as it becomes more difficult for a Westerner to understand. The Kom practice of matrilineal succession, which determined the course of my life, is byzantine in its rules and caveats, frustrating efforts at easy explanation. When a man dies his wealth, his obligations, even the ties of matrimony that have bound him to his widows pass to the first boy born to any of his sisters. If he has no sisters—as was the case with Maiyili—such wealth, obligations, and ties go to his oldest male cousin. Widows are not powerless in cases such as this. They may choose not to become the wives of this inheritor and to marry anyone they like. To do so, though, they must return a sort of reverse-dowry—the so-called "bride wealth"—that every woman's father receives when she is married. In my mother's case the sum of money involved was not great—100,000 Cameroonian francs; 50 U.S. dollars, more or less. Her father was a wealthy man and would have paid it if his daughter wished.

My mother faced two choices: pay the bride wealth back and choose a husband; or let her father keep the bride wealth, in which event she would become the wife of a ten-year-old cousin named Barnabas Afuma. The calculations for her were not simple ones to make, for benefits and disadvantages lay in either course she took. On one hand, she believed that the most important duty of her life was to bear a son—a son who would be a long time coming if she became the wife of Barnabas. On the other hand she believed, I think, that her second most important duty was to see that such a son would have a future beyond hard labor, jiggers, lice, malaria, and subsistence living—a future which, in her mind anyway, only Maiyili's family could provide.

My mother is nothing if not a determined woman—shrewd, tenacious, single-minded in the pursuit of goals that she has set herself. She saw what no one else had seen, that there was a third course available to her which could give her both the son she badly wanted and the opportunity for him to make something of his life: while remaining nominally the wife of Barnabas Afuma, and thus a member of Maiyili's family, she could bear the boy out of wedlock. The decision that my mother made in choosing this third path cannot have been an easy one, and yet, knowing her as I do, I think that it had in some ways been foreordained.

In choosing this third course she abandoned her prospects of security on behalf of the son she wished to have—a son not merely unconceived, but whose father had not yet been imagined—because she wanted to give him the advantages that would accrue while she remained a member of Maiyili's family. One can scarcely comprehend the depth of sacrifice involved with this decision. Penniless, without either husband or the prospect of getting one, without even the son for which the sacrifice was being made, my mother was left to the good offices of others in order to survive.

Following Maiyili's death, and gathering her possessions and her infant daughter in her arms, my mother began a journey that would take her from one village to the next, from Anjin to Baingo, from Baingo to Muggeff, from Muggeff to Njinikom, stopping for uncertain stays with relations who were kind enough to take her in. Along the way she met the man who would father her next two children—both, alas, lovely daughters—until at last, when she had returned once more to Anjin and was living in the compound of her father, she met Nsom Nabi, a basket weaver who would give her the single thing for which so much sacrifice was being made. I know nothing else about the man. Aside from the facts of my father's name and occupation, my mother has refused to speak of him.

I was conceived in Anjin but born at the Catholic hospital in Njinikom. My mother called me a "miracle baby," my birth a "divine intervention." But however determined my mother was in the pursuit of her goals, even she could not affect the winds of chance that blow across our lives to lead us in directions we might never have imagined. Perhaps my mother would have stayed in Anjin; perhaps my life would have taken a very different course if not for an ear infection that I contracted as an infant, which would lead us, eventually, to the hands of a traditional healer who could only be found in the village of Fungom. Thus my mother made the three-hour walk, alone except for her three girls and infant son, to that particular place. Thus she turned up on the doorstep of a particular relative—my Uncle Seing. Thus it was that I arrived in the village where my remembered life would start; the village that would nurture me; the place where I would soon believe every man to be my father, where I would chase the goats when they escaped and cut my knee at hide-and-seek.

The games I played, the paths I strolled, the people I knew in Fungom would shape the course of my existence. Such things matter, whether one believes that it is chance alone which leads us through the twists and turns of life, or that it's fate, or that, as I believe, some greater purpose shapes our destinies. For me in any case I have often thought that life might not have been so good to me had my mother not found her way to the obscure village that I have ever since called home.

There was in the village one person besides my mother and Uncle Seing who would greatly shape the course my life would take. I knew him as Uncle Diffrey. He was a tall, wiry, kindly man and an entrepreneur of sorts, who, besides his farming, bought clothes wholesale in the city of Bamenda and sold them at local markets. Uncle Diffrey was the wealthiest of my uncles. Indeed, his business had so prospered that he began to cast around for someone to help him with his burdens. I seemed a likely choice. He knew how poor my mother was, how many mouths she had to feed, how hard ready money was to come by, and so he made her a proposition: in return for my coming to live with him and helping with his work, he would pay for my education.

In that way I went to live for some six years with Uncle Diffrey and his family.

I believe my mother understood that Uncle Diffrey, as among the most decent, principled, and generous men she knew, would help to impart those qualities to me. He was the sort with whom one cannot imagine that anybody ever quarreled. I came to call him "Pa." His wife, whom I called Nawain, was quite young and very sweet to me, and his daughter, Victorine, I idolized. Victorine was five or seven years my senior, and, I thought, beautiful. I helped her with the chores. With Victorine I carried water home in calabash gourds; with her I hunted the grasshoppers on Fungom Hill, which Nawain would fry for us or boil exactly as my mother had.

At Uncle Diffrey's house we rose each day at dawn, when, as the village came to life, I fetched his goats to lead them to the fields. Weekdays after breakfast Nawain would sometimes pack a snack of fruit or bread, and off I'd set with other children to walk to Belo School. The trail ran three miles from Fungom down the slope to Sho; across a bridge of eucalyptus logs that overspread the little Ashing River; up a hill through Kichu and along a trail from which smaller paths branched off to the several village compounds. The paths were wide as they led from the centers of the villages, but soon narrowed. They were steep and rocky and filled with ruts and holes—difficult at any time and treacherous during the rainy season, when water rushed down their slopes in streams, and the mud that covered them caused one constantly to slip, spilling loads of wood, bundles of clothes, basketsful of vegetables. Our feet, though thickly calloused, were so filled with jiggers that walking was a torment. The things had deformed some children's feet, and I remember being filled even at the age of six by a great sadness at the sight of them.

The trails were not always empty. At certain hours people streamed back and forth along their winding courses, stopping to chat with their friends, waving to acquaintances, acknowledging strangers with a nod.

"Ayeah!" They would say to me. "How is your Uncle Diffrey today?"

Some days I did not go to school but instead walked this same treacherous terrain with my uncle to one market or another with a bundle of clothes balanced on my head. Each village held its market on a different day. The biggest of these, in Belo, was a chaos of merchandise in every form, of merchants, of customers, of children moving this way and that, of voices barking prices, hailing friends, bargaining with shrewd intent. Beef and bush meat could be found at the Belo market, fruits and vegetables, crayfish and sardines. Kerosene and palm oil were sold, and Vaseline and salt. I recall that one stall offered bonbons and hard candy, another medicines and bandages. Some vendors arrayed their goods on blankets spread across the ground, with umbrellas for a little shade. Some brought wooden tables on which to set their wares. Some like Uncle Diffrey took thatch-roofed stalls that shaded in the dry season but leaked terribly when rain fell in torrents from the blackened sky.

Like all Kom villages, Belo is a large, sprawling affair, the size of a New England township, and its spreading compounds with their houses, its farmland, its pastures and its woods run together in much the same way. The area around Belo is the most populous in Kom, and, outside the capital of Laikom, the most important— the place where, for example, the first missionary school had been established. Though Mother had brought me to the Belo School, we had rarely come near the market where Uncle Diffrey sold his goods, and which at first I found a little frightening: I had never seen so many people in one place before. I quickly learned to love it though. The idea that there was more to life than farming had not occurred to me. The market's air of business was infectious. The trip, though long and hard, opened the prospect of a life that had not been imagined.

"Sit and rest, Ayeah Nsom!" my uncle would say when we arrived and had finished laying out his goods in piles. As a beast of burden I was without further obligation until the time came for packing up, except to drink from the bottles of juice or water that Uncle Diffrey supplied, and to watch the swarms of people who transformed him from the retiring man whom I knew in Fungom Village into a salesman of great skill. He called out prices to the passing patrons. He laughed with friends. He joked with the children who wandered in and out among the stalls. His place of business was always tidy. He carried the best Nigerian clothes and was very proud of what he sold, and it amazed me how he seemed to know what each customer might want.

At the end of the day Uncle Diffrey would hand me an avocado or a mango that he'd reserved for the purpose, and, perhaps, make me a present of a shirt or pair of pants. He liked to sip a cup of palm wine while we tied our bundles up, or nibble on a kola nut that some friend had given him that day. On the way home we often stopped to rest at the intersection of two dirt roads. There we drank from a public water fountain and picked berries, or searched out insects to pop into our mouths. As we gathered our strength, Uncle Diffrey recounted stories of his youth, of which, he said, I frequently reminded him. He was the sort of person who values the worth of everyone he meets, and I will never forget how good he made me feel, and how appreciative he was for everything I did for him.

Among the stories told to me by Uncle Diffrey was the legend of the python that led our people from hardship and despair into the fertile land where we now lived. As with any legend, it must contain some truth. In fact, historians have determined that we Kom are among the Grassland People who, in the 18th century, drifted south from what is now Nigeria. It's true that we lived for a time together with one of these people, the Bamessi. It's true that we later immigrated to the region of savannah and mountains that we inhabit now.

The rest of the story, most of it improbable, contains those deeper truths and evidence of hope and aspiration which are, after all, the purpose of legend: that from the story our identity has acquired the nobility that is so necessary to pride, purpose, hard work, and success. In this story the Kom people are said to have prospered more than our cousins the Bamessi, with whom we had lived in harmony. The Bamessi are said to have grown jealous. Treachery soon followed in the form of a plan to exterminate our tribe.

According to this story, the Bamessi suggested one day that each tribe build its own religious house, where we might worship separately behind doors which, for unexplained reasons, were to be *locked from the outside*. We raised our church; the Bamessi raised theirs, identical in every way except for the existence of a secret tunnel that might be used for escape. For a time these religious houses were used for their intended purposes. One day, though, while the leaders of the tribes watched from a hillside as their young men knelt in prayer, both churches were set afire. The Kom perished; the Bamessi escaped.

The tale of what followed contains elements that sound so much like stories from the Bible that I've wondered whether pieces of the Christian narrative had not made their ways south from Rome or Greece or Israel. The Kom leader is said to have told his people that he would reappear one day, and shortly afterwards hanged himself. Where he died, a great lake suddenly appeared. The lake glistened. Fish swam in great numbers beneath its rippling surface, beckoning the Bamessi to catch them. But when, eagerly, the Bamessi waded in to catch these fish, the lake bottom collapsed. Something like the Egyptians who, following the Israelites, were consumed by the waters of the Red Sea, the Bamessi all drowned. An exodus of the Kom then followed as they wandered through a wilderness such as Jesus inhabited in the forty days, and starving much as Jesus starved through fasting for those weeks.

One day, when the Kom had reached the depths of weariness, hungry and desperate, a python appeared to a group of young Kom men, 25-feet long and so magnificent that the Kom knelt before it in prayer. Other Kom soon gathered to gape at the thing. The snake rose up to half its length, and then, as if offering its protection, turned to lead them to a new and better land. Though the snake soon disappeared, it left behind a deep furrow to show our people the way to the bountiful country that we would settle. Thus we found Laikom, which remains the capital of Kom, and thus our remembered history was born.

Among the lessons of this legend that Uncle Diffrey did not fail to impart was that each of us has a python trail which we must follow and from which, in following, we cannot fail to find the safe, rich, healthful country of our destinies. From time to time since that day when I first heard the story of the python I have thought of this, of the trail that I have followed through my life, and of the bright, unknown country which lies certainly ahead. The story gives me a kind of faith, not unlike my Christian faith, that my struggles will be rewarded. I have never believed that a person must have one faith alone. I continue to treasure my Kom heritage as much as I treasure my Christian one, and to see the truths that lie in such legends as our own, as well as in the magic that my mother holds so close to her. Belief in many ways is frequently its own reward.

Much of Uncle Diffrey lies in the stories that he told me. I loved his company and I recall much more than the hardship of carrying a basket on my head the beauty of the time I spent with

him. Approaching Fungom in the evening, we glimpsed Bobong
Hill rising in the distance just above our village. I can still see the
twilit people moving back and forth across that hill, some carrying
bundles, some cutting grass with sickles, some with long staffs
tending herds of grazing cattle. At home while Uncle Diffrey's
friends came around to see how he'd made out, Nawain with a
small sharp stick dug the jiggers from my feet and afterwards
brushed my tears away.

My mother had sent me to live with Uncle Diffrey to learn
responsibility, and to learn, too, how valuable are character and
honesty. For all of her ambition for her oldest son, these were the
qualities she thought most important in a man. She wanted me to
learn to treat others as I myself wanted to be treated. She wanted
me to learn that argument is self-defeating. She wanted me to be a
good and decent person—qualities which, indeed, I could not
help learning from the man.

CHAPTER THREE

While I was living with Uncle Diffrey and his family I had come to stop in Belo before and after school with a relative of my mother's late husband. Her name was Martha Nsang. She was a former primary school teacher who had married David Cheng—himself a teacher—and with him had borne a son my age named Emmanuel. As the gateway to my eventual success, Nawain Martha would become, for better and for worse, among the most influential people in my life.

Bobe David and Nawain Martha lived in a house which by Belo standards was considered fine. By the standards of my village it was a palace. Though the house was endowed with neither running water nor electricity, it did boast four bedrooms and a living room, and, in a separate building connected by a breezeway, a large kitchen. Its roof was planked with eucalyptus, which itself was overlaid with zinc. During that season when the rains blew in in waves from the west, our house in Fungom, despite its being rethatched every year, leaked like Uncle Diffrey's stall. The Cheng's house, on the other hand, remained blessedly dry.

For anyone the trip to Belo was long. For me, who had to rise at dawn and with little legs journey there in rain and mud up and down the hillsides, it was arduous. At Bobe David's and Nawain Martha's house I could rest a while before and after school. In return for meals that Nawain Martha provided, I performed light chores with their son, who, like me, was treated by his parents as a prince. I learned to call Bobe David "Sir." Martha I called "Ma." I thought them both as upright as my Uncle Diffrey was.

Bobe David taught at the Belo Primary School and was a deacon in the Baptist church who, on Sundays, stood beside the pastor to translate the English-language sermon into Kom. He was a devout man, straightforward and honest, the sort to whom people in the street nodded in respect. Martha, for her connections, for her business sense, and for the several farms she owned, also carried weight in Belo, and gave the impression in the time I spent with her of a kind and caring woman.

Then as now in Cameroon higher education was the portal through which most people passed if they wanted to move beyond a life of subsistence farming, and education was not possible without money and connections. Of the people my mother knew in the world, only one could give her son such an education. He was Andrew Ndonyi, a relative of her dead husband Maiyili, whom Maiyili had sent to university, and who thereafter became a rising star in the Cameroonian government bureaucracy. Because my mother's husband had paid for this relation's education, custom suggested that he now owed a debt to Maiyili's family—the family to which, because of my mother's sacrifice, now included me.

Andrew Ndonyi was Martha's brother and only sibling, who was now a high-ranking government official. Though I knew this personage only by reputation as "Pa Andrew," I understood that I must perform every chore with the greatest diligence in order to please the sister of the man who could determine the course of my existence. For Nawain Martha I split and stacked the firewood neatly. For her, I swept the floors with care. The dishes I washed spotlessly. The water I carried with vigilance against the possibility of spilling it. In return she fed me well and praised my work to her neighbors and her friends.

When I was ten or twelve Martha had become impressed enough with my household skills to speak to me of living there. She broached the subject casually at first, and, indeed, I could not help thinking how much the idea had to recommend: the trip from Fungom to my school each morning could take two hours; from Bobe David's and Nawain Martha's house I could make the walk in minutes. I had begun, too, to understand the importance of an education, and it was true that the long trip from my native village, as well as the work I did for Uncle Diffrey, often kept me from my classes.

Soon enough Martha began to raise more frequently the notion of my moving to their home. I debated the matter seriously. At one end or the other of my trip the answer would be clear, for I had rather stay with Uncle Diffrey than live in Belo with Bobe David, Nawain Martha, and Emmanuel. It was from time spent in the long middle of this trip—while walking in the rain, up and down the muddy hillsides often in the dark, the sounds of lurking animals on either side to frighten me—that the scales began to tip. Weekly and then almost daily Martha pestered me to move; the walk grew more tedious with every step I took. I had never mentioned her idea to Uncle Diffrey for he had been too good to me for me to think of disappointing him.

Such calculations are, I think, near the heart of human destiny: the good weighed against the bad; the selfless against the selfish; the rewards of honesty and promised labor done against convenience and opportunity. How does one resolve such calculations? Ought I not be able to continue with my education, as I would by living in Belo? Should not my future count for something? On the other hand, I must consider that a good person would do the right thing, that I was a good person, and that that goodness owed itself largely to the man whom I now meant to abandon. What would become of Uncle Diffrey's business without me to carry goods for him?

At its heart, the problem I now faced was fear. How, indeed, could I look into the eyes of a good man whom I wished to disappoint? How much I loved him! How much I owed him! What disgrace I'd feel before his gaze! Even worse, it occurred to me that there might lie in Uncle Diffrey some unknown reserve of anger and reproach that would doom my happiness.

When in time the cost of travel seemed to grow too large, I took the shameful course.

It happened one day after school while stopping at the house in Belo that my chores for Nawain Martha ran longer than was usual. The more I thought of walking home the more wearying it seemed. In time, my comfort and my future won out against my faithful obligation and I declared to her that I would stay.

In the morning I spent ten minutes on the walk to school, and, just as I'd imagined, the shortness of the trip left me in wonder at its ease. In the afternoon I stayed for extra help from my instructors, which before had been impossible. Always though with each feeling of something gained came another one of guilt. Would Uncle Diffrey worry at my absence? Would his wife? Would Victorine? Time and time again I wondered how without my help he would carry his clothes to Belo or Njinikom on market day.

Only on the weekend when I should have washed my uniform, but had no change of clothes, did Bobe David grow alarmed.

"Where are your other clothes, Ayeah?" he inquired.

"Sir, they are still at Uncle Diffrey's," I replied.

"Didn't you tell your uncle that you were going to live with us?"

"No, sir. I was afraid to ask. I thought that he might beat me and not allow me to come back."

"I will tell him and retrieve your clothes for you," Bobe David said.

"No, Sir, please don't."

Martha came into the room.

Her husband turned to her.

"Mama, Ayeah has not told his family that he's staying here."

"It doesn't matter, David," Martha answered. "Let him stay here with us."

But Bobe David did not want my family to worry.

"Ayeah," he said. "You must return home and tell your uncle. Is this what you really want to do?"

Mama was adamant.

"Of course he wants to stay with us. He can go to secondary school. My brother is already making plans for him. He has no choice now! He has chores to do!"

"Ayeah, Son," Bobe David continued patiently. "Is this really what you want?"

"Yes, Sir," I replied.

He smiled.

"It is settled then. Tomorrow morning, go back to Fungom and tell your uncle where you've been. Gather your clothes and return to us. Make sure to explain why it is you're leaving. He will understand. He's a good man."

Martha did not want me to return to Fungom. I would come to learn that she had never cared for me, for my comfort or condition. She would within a day or two begin to treat me strictly as a servant, and look at me only in terms of the work that I could do. Why let me go back to Fungom, she doubtless thought, when there was sweeping to be done? Why risk the chance that Uncle Diffrey would not permit me to move to Belo yet?

Reluctantly, though, she agreed with the decision of her husband. I suppose she had no choice.

"Yes, Ayeah that will be the right thing," she said. "Now, go and finish up your chores."

I did not sleep that night as I contemplated my return to Fungom. My fear grew hourly. And though I tried to imagine as Bobe David urged what words would best explain my desire to move, none appeared to me.

I rose at first light, while a few stars could still be seen to glimmer in the western sky. With two avocados and a bottle of water I set out.

By now I had made the walk to Fungom so frequently that I knew every root, every rock, every hole along the way as well as I knew my hands and feet. That morning, though, these same roots and rocks forsook our close association. They sprang to life, attacking me, it seemed, with malignant intent. I tripped. I fell. I skinned my knees and elbows. The nearer I drew to Uncle's house the more frightened I became. He whom I knew as a sweet and decent man grew ominous and ugly. Though I had never had a beating at his hand, I now imagined one. I felt already the shame that his rebuke would bring. Perhaps he would not let me go. Perhaps my schooling would soon end. Perhaps I was destined forever to carry clothes for him.

The sun was up when I reached the outskirts of my village. The path slowly widened. At Uncle Diffrey's house I found that all was quiet. Indeed, as far as I could see no one seemed to be about. Dare I hope that I might fetch my things and leave before anyone appeared?

I tiptoed to the bedroom where my clothes were kept. The bag I packed was small. I came, I went as silently as possible, and soon was walking quietly down the path whence I had traveled there. How relieved I was to have missed the man entirely. And yet though I had escaped the anger of Uncle Diffrey and the beating that must follow, I found myself uneasy at my luck. The guilt I felt at leaving him was traded for the guilt of running off. How indifferent I would seem to him for all that he had done; how thankless for his many kindnesses. So too as my shame grew was I saddened by my loss.

"Who is that?" someone called out suddenly.

It was Uncle Diffrey, who at that moment had walked around the corner of his house.

"Is that you, Ayeah?" he inquired.

I was mortified.

"Yes, Uncle—yes, it's me."

"Come back and tell me where you're going," he said to me in the sternest voice that I had ever heard from him.

I hung my head.

"Uncle, please," I replied in my most pitiable manner. "I am going to live in Belo, close to school. Bobe David and Martha want me to stay and work for them. I can finish school Pa, and go to secondary school as well."

"Ayeah, Ayeah—I was worried about you. We all were."

I stopped shaking for a time and found the courage to look up at him.

He grew silent. He shifted his weight from one foot to the other.

At last he walked up to me.

"I knew this day would come," he said. "I just did not think that it would be so soon."

He laid his hand on my shoulder.

"What is in that bag?" he asked.

"My clothes, Pa."

"Hmmmm," he said.

For a moment neither of us spoke as we considered the consequences of this new arrangement in our lives.

"Why did you not tell me you were leaving?" he asked.

"Uncle . . . ," I began.

But he knew why. I was a boy still, in the body of a man.

"Ayeah, I am very proud of you," he told me at last. "You have done much for me and you have learned well. I want you to finish school. There is much to learn still and while I would love to have you with me always, I would rather see you follow your own path as I have followed mine. Bobe David is a good man. Do your best for him and his family as you have done for me."

We had so much love, each one for the other, that we both came close to tears.

"Run along, Ayeah," he said. "Good luck with school and make me proud."

He shook my hand. I left. I looked back once or twice to see him standing by his house, watching as I disappeared.

CHAPTER FOUR

Belo by the standards of my native village was cosmopolitan. Even before I went to live with Bobe David and Nawain Martha I knew this to be true from my visits there with Uncle Diffrey. Still, it is difficult for someone not native to such a remote corner of the world to understand how a child working at a market might have failed to pay much attention to a fifth part of the town in which it stood. I knew well only the section where my uncle sold his clothes. The vegetables, the fruits, the meats, the breads—these meant little to me then; I rarely even looked at them. I had never stayed in Belo after dark, and so had not seen Belo's single light bulb, which ran on a generator and lit the largest bar in town. We did not go into bars. I had never entered Belo's only rest-house, or noticed either the travelers who stopped there or the prostitutes who served them. The barber shops and hairdressers, the tailors, the repairers of watches and the menders of shoes—these had remained invisible to me until I began to live with David, Martha, and Emmanuel.

Most astonishing to me was the discovery of things that moved at great speeds along the roads. They came in two varieties—described to me as Land Cruisers and Land Rovers—and were said to have been made by a people called "Americans." The vehicles sent dust plumes soaring to the sky or splashed through muddy ruts. Their drivers resting elbows on the doors were carefree in a sense that I had never known the word, and appeared to me at that time as being at the zenith of sophistication. I vowed that one day I myself would drive; that I would hold my arm just so and give that same look of worldliness.

If the market stood as the commercial center of the village, the complex of buildings where I went to school was its religious, medical, and intellectual. These buildings included besides the primary school which I had attended since the age of four, the Baptist church of which Bobe David was a deacon, and the so-called Maternity Center, whose function on the scale of medical establishments lay just below that of an infirmary. Babies were born at the Maternity Center and medicines dispensed, but only midwives—both American and Kom—could be found there. The church, to which these institutions owed their existence, had been founded in 1936 by a German-American missionary, Paul Gebauer, though it was now run by Kom.

In Belo it wasn't the technologies alone that fascinated me, but the reports of those as yet unseen. Though there was one light bulb in the town, I heard from here and there that by the thousands such bulbs lighted entire cities. No telephone existed in Belo, yet people told me that it was possible to speak to friends and relatives at great distances. In the aeroplanes, I myself might aspire one day to fly.

Despite the magical technologies in Belo, my time spent there was not an altogether happy one. The trucks I saw were nice; the friends I made were good; Bobe David was a kind and decent man; his son Emmanuel, who went to school with me, often helped me with my chores. But all of these things even taken together were scarcely balanced by my unhappiness at living beneath the stern hand of Nawain Martha. If she had managed in the time I lived with Uncle Diffrey to mask her customary disposition, she did not bother after I came to live with her. The change in her attitude towards me was startling. Indeed, she was of a type that I had never seen in Fungom—dominant, possessive, jealous and mercurial.

In Belo besides the ire of Martha Cheng I discovered the existence of night creatures worse than any I had known before. The scorpions, the snakes, the spiders seemed larger than the ones in Fungom. The juju were reported by everyone I knew to be more terrifying. What was worse, I learned that dead people walked about in Belo after dark, searching out the living to satisfy their appetites. This to me was the single fact which gave me to know that Belo was a more frightening place to be at night than was my little village. No dead people had ever walked about in Fungom.

I was a more fearful boy than most, I think, and it was this fear which led to my first mistreatment at Nawain Martha's hands. She had given me when I moved into her house a bedroom of my own, a bed, and bedding for me to lie upon. It was incredible to think that such a space was mine alone: I had never in my life known anything like privacy. Still, there was no sort of bathroom in the house. By day I walked outside to urinate. At night I faced two choices: I either ventured out into that dark world where the juju, ghosts, and zombies were waiting with their grim intent, or I wet my bed. The equation was a simple one to solve. For bedwetting I was scolded by the mistress of the house. Still, I could not help myself, and wet the bed again. It wasn't long before Nawain Martha had had enough of that, and banished me forever to the kitchen where until the age of 16 I slept like Cinderella by the hearth.

I became for Martha the hired hand. I cleaned the house. I cleared the dinner plates and washed the dishes, pots, and pans. I gathered firewood and stacked it. I hauled water from the mighty

Mughom River, which, though not clean enough to drink, was clean enough for cooking. In the Mughom too I washed the family's clothes, sometimes next to girls from my school who worked beside their mothers.

Martha often criticized my work.

"These pots will need to be scrubbed well after dinner!" she would say. "I have not been at all impressed with your work lately!"

"I will clean them, Mama," I'd reply.

If I did not perform my chores according to her expectations I might get no more than a crust of bread to eat and half a cup of tea to drink. Nawain sometimes denied me food altogether, so that I was forced to beg my supper from the neighbors. The neighbors were always kind to me. They knew Martha for the shrew she was and sympathized with me. Her wrath was legendary. Sometimes when she thought my work inadequate she refused for days to speak to me. The neighbors shook their heads and rolled their eyes.

The weekends were especially unpleasant because Bobe David saved the Seventh Day for rest. In order to prepare the food that we would need for Sundays, I worked unceasingly from Friday evening until Sunday morning grinding corn and pounding coco-yams, shelling beans and peeling fruit. On the Sabbath despite its being kept I had, besides attending church, two chores. In the morning it was I who cooked breakfast for the house. In the afternoon I was often sent to market to sell the puff-puff bread that Martha baked. This treat was made from corn flour and sugar, and fried in palm oil. But though the job of selling puff-puff wasn't difficult, I found it loathsome and demeaning. The market stalls for prepared foods occupied a section of their own, and until my arrival its breads and stews had been sold without exception by mothers and their daughters. It was they and not the men who snickered as I traded bread for coins.

Martha would never have thought to send her son to sell puff-puff at market. Emmanuel had fewer chores than I. He got more food, sometimes eating from his mother's bowl. He had his own room, where, late at night while I was working in the kitchen, he studied by the lantern light whose trail I observed with bitterness. I myself never had the time for study, and read whatever work was left for home during my classes at the school.

If I showed signs of reluctance to sell the puff-puff or perform my other chores, Nawain Martha might not only scold, but report me to her husband. When my work was finished I fell in bed exhausted, and even then could not put the woman entirely from my mind. Sometimes in the dark I could hear her faint voice speaking to her husband: Richard has not performed quickly enough or well enough; he's lazy; he never will succeed; he's not half the boy that Emmanuel is. At last, without the will or energy to move, I fell asleep to the crunching sounds of the termites who had taken refuge in the bamboo supports from which the house was made. I often thought of these tiny busy lives—that theirs like mine, were filled with hard, unceasing work, unappreciated by any human soul.

Martha was wealthy for a woman at that time and place, who had brought to her marriage with David Cheng plots of land in Baingo, Mbingo, Ashing, and Njinikejem. Her primary occupation and chief means of support was tending to these farms, which lay as much as an hour's walk away, over the same sort of difficult terrain which I had walked each day from Fungom. I well knew Martha's farms, for I began to help her cultivate them. One could not fault the woman for her own work ethic. She was an avid farmer who planted, weeded, and harvested alongside those of us whom she enlisted to the cause.

Two sorts of crops grow in Kom: coffee, which brings the most money for the labor spent and whose cultivation is the province of men alone; and every other crop, which both men and women grow. Corn is the main cash crop for those who can sell it at the market. Sometimes I alone accompanied Martha to her farms. At other times, and during the harvest especially, my friends from school would join us.

We trundled Martha's baskets on our heads, uphill and down. These baskets rested on small wreaths of braided grass that helped to cushion, as well as balance them. I could carry the baskets with my arms swinging at my sides, though I never learned as others did to do so with a calabash of water in each hand. Not infrequently while carrying the corn I stubbed my toe on rocks or stepped into a hole and fell. At such times the thought of rising was so exhausting that I sometimes sat awhile and cried.

Long days of work were usual, as they were for everyone I knew. And yet despite Nawain Martha's mistreatment, my time in Belo was not entirely miserable. I did enjoy games of soccer. We played in the dusty roads with balls made of rolled-up banana leaves, and thought nothing of making passersby stand and wait for us. I liked learning. I liked the rhythms of the school day, and afterwards to play in the river with my best friends, Grace and Solomon, catching minnows, crawfish, crabs. Among the times that I remember best were the evenings spent in snaring crickets, which, in the rainy season, emerged from their holes to rub their wings in song. Hunting crickets was not at all like catching grass-hoppers. It required, instead of fevered snatching, cunning patience. My friends and I stole into the fields at night equipped with lanterns, pouches, and a sort of machete that we called cutlasses.

In my memory the crickets in Belo were more numerous, their din more incredible than any I have heard since then. When, after dusk, the things began to chirp, they sounded like a choir. I imagined them moving from their holes and speaking to their kin, and wondered too whether the poor creatures were destined to sing themselves like thorn birds to their deaths. Once among them I raised my lantern to illuminate their shadows, and, finding a likely victim, crept closer. I shone the light into its eyes so that, startled, it would freeze. I slammed my cutlass by its hole to cut off its escape. I grabbed the insect by its neck and put it in my pouch. At home we ate them, fried or boiled.

Celebrations also took my mind away from the hardships that I faced. The most joyous of these took place at the births of babies—celebrations with which I was intimately familiar as a resident in Belo. As the location of the Belo Maternity Center, Belo drew expectant mothers from villages for miles around—as far away, in fact, as Abuh, where David Cheng got his first job as a teacher. The trip from Abuh was so arduous that David invited its mothers to stop with us during their last few days of pregnancy. It was I whom, when a birth had been announced, he would send to deliver the happy news. The trip to Abuh took four hours by paths that led across the most difficult terrain that I had known, past Njinikom, across several swiftly flowing streams, and, most significantly, up Yang Hill—a rise of 2,600 feet from valley floor—and through the royal compound in Laikom, the capital of Kom.

I have returned to Laikom since that first visit. It sits above the clouds. Its views are spectacular, for the world so far as one can tell from there is made of mountain peaks and valleys covered with bright green trees—yellowwood and ironwood, waterberry, elders. The vistas, indeed, are not unlike those which one has from the mountaintops of my adopted Maine. Neither lights nor houses nor farms nor any other sign of humankind can be seen from there.

I had little time on my youthful journeys to appreciate the beauty of the place, as, weary and sweating, my feet disturbed by jiggers, I made my way across the mountaintop. But though the trip was long and hard, still it was more than made up for by the joy with which my news was greeted. At the sight of me, who always brought the news, the women of the village gave a special call reserved for births alone, which brought villagers from their farms and compounds a mile away or more. Women in the village grasped me in their arms, hugging me tightly and kissing me, and asking questions about the newborn which I was not prepared to answer, because, as I'd explain, I hadn't seen the baby yet. A celebration began which would last three days or more. The women sang songs of gratitude and danced. Special meals were cooked. The men, dressed in flamboyant native costumes, brought bush meat to the affair, and the children, whose usual fare was meager, gorged themselves.

The trip was so long and difficult that I always spent the night. I was treated like royalty. Proud fathers gave me spending money—500 Cameroonian francs or more—and a present of the palm oil that was passed out as a traditional gift to everyone on occasions such as that.

I enjoyed myself immensely at these times. Once though, I recall, I had to carry to Abuh the news of a still-birth, which weighed terribly on me as I made the trek. The women who began to rejoice at the sight of me were shocked, and as the news was passed, began to wail. The keening never stopped, even as I tried to sleep, and I remember that night as being among the saddest of my life. In Belo ever after that, I never saw the mothers coming there in the same light as I had viewed them earlier. Healthy births, which before I took for granted, were more precious now; life was more precarious.

The invitation for these mothers to stay with us was Bobe David's gift, and an indication of his character. Beyond such celebrations, beyond the school, the games, the hunting of the crickets, the fishing for tadpoles with my friends, it was he who made life in Belo tolerable. David and Martha were so different that I'm quite sure many people in the village wondered how they could stay conjoined in holy matrimony. Where Martha was loud, scolding, and judgmental, David was reserved and kind. Where she, though confessing piety, was calculating, where she spoke ill of others when they'd turned their backs, her husband practiced the virtues that he preached.

He was an imposing figure who stood over six feet tall. Children feared him when they passed him in the road, merely out of awe. His positions as a teacher and a deacon were among the village's most respected jobs. I often thought he carried himself not unlike a prophet. He had a distinctive way of walking too, one hand inside a trousers pocket and pulling up on it as if about to draw a coin out, that somehow enhanced for me the greatness of his image.

He was a strict disciplinarian, tidy in his habits. I had several jobs, among them to shine his shoes each morning, to clear his plate the moment he had finished eating, and to clean the room that served as his office. I tried my best to please him, not merely for the promise of my further education, but from respect. When, though, I lapsed in performing tasks to his high standards—and especially early on when, at 10 or so, I had just moved in with them—he beat me as any father in the neighborhood would.

Though it was Martha through her brother who held the key to my future, it was David who bought my school books, my uniform, the first pair of trousers that I owned. It was he too who one Sunday before we left for church presented me with a gift that nearly took my breath away. This was a common pair of Nigerian rubber shoes—the first shoes that I had ever owned—whose benefits, as I would learn, were nearly outweighed by the stink they produced when worn by sweaty feet, and their propensity to fall apart.

David was a Christian in the best sense of the word, a father and a mentor who treated me with the respect he gave Emmanuel. He taught us Christian songs and in the evenings assembled the family in the living room to read the Bible, to reflect upon our day, to learn what lessons the Good Book offered, and to pray. He preached the message that God would give us hope in troubled times, the strength to live hard lives. Just as we derived strength from the power of community, in other words—the strength we took from the sharing of school snacks, from giving our labor to help our neighbors on their farms—so now, we understood, such strength would be supported by the hand of God.

His favorite of the apostles was Paul, the Jew and Roman citizen whose conversion is among the most important in the Christian faith. Paul founded churches across Europe and Asia Minor. He's credited with writing nearly half the books in the New Testament. It's St. Paul's philosophy of atonement—that Christians are redeemed from sin by Jesus's death and resurrection—which lies at the heart of Christianity. Of all Paul's messages, though, the one that I remember David preaching most was the faith that Paul himself had learned from perseverance through his many hardships—that ". . . forgetting those things which are behind, and reaching forth unto those things which are before, I press toward the mark for the prize of the high calling of God in Christ Jesus."

It's the message that my mother often preached to me, the advice which I have taken most to heart, and which has served me at the lowest moments of my life.

The Belo Baptist Church, where we marched each Sunday without fail, was the heart of our community. It occupied a single floor and rested on a mud and brick foundation. Its ceiling was higher than any ceiling I had known. On one side sat the women and girls; on the other the men and boys. The pastor preached in English, one phrase at a time, and waited as Bobe David put the message into Kom. I loved the rituals of church, the spirit of community, the focus of devotion, the message of Christ's sacrifice for all.

Since coming to Belo at the age of four to attend its primary school, I had learned a great deal about the life of Jesus Christ on earth. I learned that He had walked on water; that He had calmed the storm; that He had turned water into wine. Indeed, so well did I know Jesus that I had no doubt I could have pointed Him out if He passed me on the street. There was in the school's devotional hall a flip chart containing the images of Jesus Christ and Satan—a chart which, from being worn and dirty, reminded me of the countless students who had flipped its pages long before I saw them. Christ was a white man with long blond hair and eyes of the deepest blue. Satan on the other hand was, like me, quite black. Satan had pointy ears and a long curling tail, and could be seen carrying a pitchfork. I believed myself absolutely to be as evil as I imagined the pictured Satan to be, a conviction which, I should say, made salvation an all the more urgent proposition.

One Sunday morning after church I came as usual into the churchyard to mingle with the gathered crowd. Here and there as outside every Christian church following a service, people chatted with their friends. One group especially caught my eye for being larger than the rest. I soon saw why. People whom I recognized from Belo and surrounding villages were speaking to a white man and a white woman, the first that I had ever seen. The man I knew certainly to be Jesus Christ. The woman I more vaguely recognized as Eve. The idea that Christ Himself had come to stand in the yard of the Belo Baptist Church stunned me. I remember well how I trembled, and how my soul seemed to fill with more goodness than any I could ever have imagined. For a moment, I believe, my breathing even ceased. I stared in open wonderment.

It would never have occurred to me to approach the two. In Kom culture, children do not speak to adults without having first been spoken to; it's taboo even to look a grownup in the eyes. Beyond such matters, though, I was certain, from observing Satan on the walls of the devotional hall, that my skin was unclean, and that if I touched the hands of these divinities my hand would dirty theirs.

I did hang about, though, watching the couple for as long as they remained. In time I took myself home and couldn't wait to tell the great man, the deacon and the teacher who was the head of our family of the miracle that I had seen.

Just as it's taboo in Kom to look a grownup in the eye, so too is it taboo to call any of them by their names. If the women are called "Nawain," the men are addressed uniformly as "Sir."

So excited was I though, from the sight which I had witnessed, that I forgot my good manners.

"Bobe David, Bobe David!" I cried as I rushed into the house. "I have seen Jesus! I have seen Jesus!"

And though David explained to me that Jesus had long since ascended into heaven and that no one on earth could see Him anymore, I refused to hear it. I told Nawain Martha and Emmanuel that I had seen the Lord. I told my friends as well. It would be a long time, in fact, before I would not have sworn that every white man I came across was the embodiment of Jesus Christ.

CHAPTER FIVE

Not long after seeing Jesus in the yard of the Belo Baptist Church, I began to see Him and other Jesuses everywhere I went. These holy men for example seemed to frequent a section of the market where food was sold, and which, until I had settled with David and Martha, I had never paid attention to. I saw Jesuses on the road, here on foot, there in their trucks bouncing up and down the rutted roads. Again I saw Christ attending services at church. Soon enough I learned that He as well as all the Eves that walked about the earth congregated in the largest numbers at the Maternity Center, to which the expectant mothers of Abuh and other villages came when it was time.

As part of the compound of buildings that included both my school and the church, the Maternity Center too was central to our community. It was among the nicest buildings in the area. Its walls were made of cement. In its yard stood a tap which gave the only drinking water within ten miles—never running dry; free to all. The center was a busy place. I myself was treated there for fevers, stomachaches, and other maladies. Once when a rock fell on my toe the midwives at the center bandaged it for me. We had to keep a notebook in which these midwives made entries of the illnesses for which they'd treated us. The women were very strict on this point, and would not attend to you if you failed to present them with the book.

The midwives were mostly in their thirties. Though the majority had come from Belo and surrounding villages, there were at all times one or two Americans who lived in a nice brick house and served to train the Kom who came to work there. The white women were highly intelligent, as I could tell from their blue eyes and their long blond hair, which I wanted desperately to touch. They were pretty enough, I guess, but it was their whiteness and not their beauty which interested me. I used any excuse to find myself in their vicinity. I played soccer on the road that passed the center by. I fetched water from the tap and gathered firewood that lay scattered thereabouts. Orange, mango, and guava trees abounded near the place, and plantain and kola trees. These provided excellent cover from which to view the scene. With Nawain Martha's fury in mind I hid for as long as I dared behind these tree trunks among the fallen fruit, watching the white people come and go.

"Is that Jesus Christ?" I would ask myself when one of them walked by. They didn't frighten me. I watched them with open mouth and smiled at the idea of them. I laughed with joy to behold such visions right before my eyes, and wished that I could be like them.

These divinities never noticed me. I was merely one among a dozen boys who might at any time be hanging about the place. My clothes were often dirty, my feet deformed from jiggers. My nose often dripped; mucous dried on my upper lip. I had little English anyway, and could not have talked to them even if I'd dared.

The Jesuses and Eves whom I so devoutly watched were all said to come from a country called America, and themselves to be a people called Americans. The Mr. Muller who sometimes came to church, and who, I later learned, had fled the Nazis in the

1930s, was to me American. The white men who worked on the
Belo Water Project and dined at our house with David Cheng—
these, though they undoubtedly included Europeans, I knew to be
Americans. My friends, my relatives explained that Americans
were responsible for everything that awed me in the world. I believed that the Creator had endowed them with supernatural powers. The trucks that plied our rutted roads, the bulldozers that
maintained them—these were manufactured exclusively by
Americans. Who had made the planes that passed overhead? Who
flew them? In each case, Americans. Who had made the watch
that could tell time? Who had made the radio that Bobe David
acquired, that talked like magic? Americans all.

Not long after I moved to Belo I was introduced to an even
more incredible technology—this too created by Americans. For
though there was no television in Belo at that time, there was a
single television set and a VCR on which could be played tapes of
American television shows. This miracle was owned by a family
who lived on the Belo Market Square. Its shows could be seen
through a window of the family's house, so that we kids gathered
constantly there, pushing and shoving each other to get a better
view of life as it was lived so far away.

The Cosby Show I watched with wonder. Michael Jackson
moonwalked on a stage and John Travolta, whose photo was emblazoned on a t-shirt I had bought, danced with Karen Gorney
time and time again.

America was everything; soon enough I dreamt of going there.
It's hard to say why certain things in life will catch our fancies and,
in time, will shape our lives. The fabulous technologies believed to
have been created by Americans certainly impressed my friends.
The white skin of the midwives fascinated everyone I knew. Fascinated—and yet, not quite filled with wonder. No one who might

once have thought all whites to be Jesus incarnate on this earth maintained this belief as long as I. The dream of going to America took hold of no one as deeply as it soon took hold of me.

The desire to travel to America, though it dawned on me slowly, would in time grow with such intensity that no day passed without my calling it to mind. It became the single most important force that urged me to success, that made me work in school to the limits of my ability, that provided me the will to suffer all that Nawain Martha could throw at me. If anything, the abuse of Nawain Martha became a motivation to leave the world of Belo for that other, better place.

The idea in time possessed me. Wanting to see where the fabulous beings had come from, and despite my inability to swim, I asked if I could swim there. No, I was told. America and Cameroon were divided by a big water, which itself was filled with fish that would eat anyone who tried. Ah, I thought. I must learn geography. I wished to be the driver of trucks, who held his elbow on the door and drove so casually with one hand. I wanted to be a pilot of the planes. I wanted to be the mechanic who fixed these things. I wanted to become a teacher. I acquired in addition to my John Travolta shirt one with Michael Jackson's picture printed on its front. I began to wear a wristwatch, even though it didn't work.

Like every aspiring immigrant, I believed the streets of America to be paved with gold. Fancy cars, beautiful women, skyscrapers such as I could not conceive though I had seen them on TV, houses like the one where the Cosby family lived—these were America to me. It followed then, rather quickly I recall, not just that I might travel to the magic place, but that this was my destiny. At first from superstition, I suppose—from the sense that those I told would mock me, and that this and other unknown powers would keep me from my goal—I did not make mention of my dream.

It happened soon enough, though, that the Baptist church which was so important to my life became involved in my desire to see America, and gave me the confidence to speak my dream aloud.

Soon after moving to Belo I was asked by the pastor of our church whether I was ready to be baptized. I had no opinion on the matter.

"What is a Christian, Ayeah?" the pastor asked.

In my experience a Christian was anyone who had taken, in addition to his native name, a Christian one. My mother had a Christian name—Theresia. So did David, Martha, and Emmanuel.

But no. The pastor explained that a Christian was someone who had accepted Jesus as his savior; that to do so required time, lessons, study, and thought; and that only then—when one understood what a Christian was—could one be baptized as a Christian.

Well then, that was good, I thought. I would be baptized!

At home I was thrilled to inform Bobe David of this latest development in my religious education—that our pastor, a man of great faith and learning, had asked me if I wished to begin the process of my entering fully to the church and that I'd agreed at once. But though I had imagined Bobe's beaming ear to ear at news of my decision, I was surprised at his stern look and by the seriousness of the conversation that ensued.

In our kind of Christianity, he explained, we did not believe in baptism at birth. For us the ritual was a public display, to show the world that we'd accepted Christ, and was therefore a commitment of the sort that babies could not make. And if the ritual required a process of learning and indoctrination, the decision to embark upon this process itself required serious reflection, and private consultation with God.

"You do understand," he said, "that when you accept Jesus as your savior, you become a Christian and child of the Lord, Jesus Christ?"

"Yes sir," I replied. "I do."

"You will have the opportunity for eternal life and will become a servant of the Lord. You will be responsible for upholding the teachings of the Bible and for demonstrating publicly your commitment to him."

"Yes sir, I know."

"I feel inside that you are ready, and have been ready for some time now. You have seen much in your life. You've traveled from home to home, all the while serving others. Without even the training of the church, you have been a disciple of the teachings of the Bible from something inside you, in your heart. I would be very proud of you to accept Jesus into your life. You're a good person and I feel as close to you as if you were my own son."

"Thank you, sir."

I remember clearly the feeling of warmth that those words of Bobe David filled me with, at the thought that he should have such concern for my welfare and such faith in my character and commitment.

I remember too the tears that filled my eyes.

The decision was soon made. In time, as the process of education began, I was told that I would need to choose my Christian name. Unlike the idea of baptism, I had long considered what this name should be. Everyone had. It was the name which outside one's family one would be called for the rest of his life. For a time I considered "Samson" or "David" as suitable for the purpose, since these names connoted strength and the ability to conquer giants.

It was another name, though, which, recurring to me time and time again, at last felt most right. The president of the United States at that time bore the Christian name of Richard, and though I had no idea what a Nixon was, I had long ago learned the meaning of the word "rich." So it followed that a person whose name contained this word must himself be rich, and, that, therefore, the name itself, together with the prestige of its belonging to the president of America, would lend its weight to my dream of getting there. With such a name I could not help being destined to find my way to the country of the supernatural beings; destined for another future than the one which awaited if I never left.

With my new name on the appointed day, and in my finest clothes, I listened to the pastor preach on the subject of baptism. With it I heard our choir in song, and particularly the voice of a woman, Charlotte Church, which even now can stir me in my memory of it. With my new name I was led in a parade through waiting throngs, for four miles down the road to that place on the Mughom River where the sacred rite would be performed. The pastor held my nose and placed a palm behind my head, and brought me backwards until the muddy water covered me. He lifted me up. He handed me a towel with which to wipe my face. I saw my mother clapping and weeping, raising her voice in thankful praise.

From that day I began slowly to reveal to my relatives and other acquaintances pieces of my dream to go to the land whence Christian names had come. My friends began not infrequently to call me "Richard Nixon," a habit I encouraged. So apparent was my determination to reach that place which produced the magic things, that these same friends even called me "America." These names were a reminder of my dream, and in a strange way made me feel already an American, already a pilot and a driver of cars, a dweller in fine houses, a wearer of wristwatches that could tell time. Richard Nixon in his way had already made me rich.

CHAPTER SIX

One day when I had lived in Belo for a year or so, I learned that Pa Andrew would make a visit to our house.

This was the man for whose influence my mother had denied herself so much—a husband and security, a house and lands to call her own, her children's legitimacy. For reasons unknown to me, my mother's husband Maiyili had paid for Pa Andrew's education at the prestigious Technical College in Ombe. Pa Andrew therefore felt an obligation to return the favor to any member of Maiyili's family—a family of which, owing to my mother's decision not to remarry, I was a part.

He was the man who could help me find my way to America.

So long had I heard stories of Pa Andrew, and so essential was his help, that I could scarcely credit the news that he was coming and began to think of little else. From friends and relatives I had learned one fact about the man besides his government position that confirmed his importance: he had traveled to the country where the white people lived, which I assumed to be America. As I would later learn, Pa Andrew's prominence was not exaggerated. He *had* studied in America, at the University of Vermont. He was Cameroon's Director of Community Development and the general manager of our region's Development Authority. He traveled frequently to Europe—to Switzerland, where he liked to ski, and to Great Britain. He lived in splendid houses provided by the government, and had a car and driver to carry him about.

The importance of her brother's visit had not been lost on Nawain Martha. She planned a meal of cocoyams with fish, fufu dumplings, boiled rice, and a stew which would serve as well for Sunday's lunch.

Pa Andrew's arrival at our house awed me. He was a huge man, tall, powerfully built, and had the large belly with which we all associated the rich and powerful. His head was bald; his arms were hairy; his voice was a rich, deep bass. Indeed, the man possessed exactly the charisma that I had long imagined when I thought of him.

I was little more than skin and bones from lack of food, and stood before him shyly.

He called me "Richard."

"Richard," he said. "Mama tells me that you want to go to secondary school."

I cannot say why she'd told this to her brother unless my presence in her house could not be otherwise explained.

"Yes, Sir," I replied.

"I can use someone to help me in Buea and I have my eye on you."

"Yes, Sir."

With his encouragement all that I had pinned my hopes on, but which until now had been more a fantasy than anything, seemed tangible. I would work even harder, I told myself. I would suffer Martha without complaint. I would renew my dedication to my studies so as to meet whatever unspoken requirements Pa Andrew had for helping me.

I smiled to myself when he told his sister how skinny I looked, and that she ought to feed me well that night. She did, too. I believe that I ate more that evening than I had eaten since moving to her house. Pa Andrew and David dined alone, and I took some sly satisfaction in the fact that Martha was relegated to eating in the kitchen with Emmanuel and me—her lazy, tiresome, bastard servant.

CHAPTER SEVEN

Despite my fervor to reach America, I had for some years failed to resolve the question of how I, whose skin was black, would be treated once I got there. Bill Cosby and Michael Jackson were celebrities, and so, as I supposed, exempted from discrimination. But what of everybody else? If the evidence from my association with white people in Belo were any indication, black people always worked for them. What, I'd often wondered, would be my own fate when I made my way across the big water?

An answer to these questions arrived in Belo from the sky.

One day at school our teacher announced the planned arrival of something called a helicopter, which, as we were told, was something like an aeroplane, and which would carry our pastor and other village notables to a religious conference. I and every other student in the class were stunned by this revelation. None of us had ever heard the word before, let alone seen a helicopter. Aeroplanes, though magical, were nevertheless known objects. But now there existed in the world a machine that flew by means of blades spinning overhead. I was too shy to ask the many questions that this announcement evoked in me. Not so my classmates, though. They wished to know who had made the helicopter and where it would be flying from. How many people did it carry? Who would be driving it? Our teachers, who were as amazed by the idea of a helicopter as we students were, could not satisfy our curiosity. They did know one thing, though: that the helicopter was to land in the middle of our soccer pitch. Since we were in the middle of the dry season, and since a helicopter's blades kicked up great clouds of dust, we would have to carry water from the Mughom River to spread upon the field.

Nearly as astonishing to me as the fact that I would see this magical bird was my understanding of the landing's purpose: that white people—Americans, in other words—were coming to fetch Kom of my acquaintance the way a chauffeur arrives to pick his master up. Long after the helicopter had come and gone I puzzled over the idea that the roles of whites and blacks might be reversed from those which I had known for years to be the rule.

News of the helicopter's arrival was not confined to the Belo Primary School. That afternoon word of the event began to spread—first to the parents and siblings of my classmates, and, in short order, from them to relatives and friends. Within a day or two there could have hardly been a soul within a day's walk who had not heard of it. For a week the helicopter was the chief topic of conversation not only in our classroom but in every home, at every market stall, on every corn row and mountain path. At the churches throughout Kom, committees were organized for the helicopter's reception and sermons were preached on the subject of its mission.

I can hardly express the sense of excitement that filled us on the appointed day. It had been decided that beside wetting our field we should lay a fire to serve as a beacon for the helicopter's pilot. To this end, as the girls trudged back and forth between the Mughom River and our school, we boys scoured the landscape for firewood. We performed our tasks with a great sense of purpose and without complaint, for no work in our lives had ever seemed more worthwhile.

So too as we prepared the ground for this event did residents from near and far begin to make their way to Belo and our school. The shopkeepers in the Belo Market dropped their shades and shut their stalls; the farmers in the fields laid down their hoes. By the dozen at first, then by the score, and, soon enough, by the hundreds, the curious made their ways to the environs of the field where the helicopter was to land. The ill, the lame, the young, the old all came. Pregnant mothers held older children by the hand and carried toddlers on their shoulders. The youthful climbed mango, pear, and guava trees to get a better view; the less enterprising jostled for space beside the field. By afternoon a thousand people had arrived to stand shoulder to shoulder on the surrounding hillsides to see the thing about which so much fuss was being made, as if awaiting the arrival of a prophet.

In time the bird appeared—a tiny thing at first, flying through a cleft between two of Baingo's hills, across the empty space above Njinikejem and Kichu, at last above the enormous eucalyptus trees that flanked our field. While the school band played, our drummers keeping time, we sang songs of praise and joy. The thing grew larger and louder, until its sound deafened us. It hovered, menacing and beautiful, the word "HeliMission" emblazoned on its side. The power of its blades and the dust that rose despite our wetting of the field, which forced us to shut our eyes, were greater than anything that I had ever known. I could soon see that the helicopter's pilot was a white man, a fact that seemed to me as nearly inconceivable as the thing itself. Such a man, I thought, must be filled with unearthly powers to have come from so great a distance in such a fabulous conveyance for the benefit of men I knew.

My neighbors on the hillsides cheered the helicopter's landing. Its door opened. White missionaries emerged to shake the hands of our religious leaders. They smiled. They waved to us. For an hour they remained there on our dusty soccer field, chatting with the dignitaries, greeting the curious, watching as my friends and neighbors swarmed around the helicopter to peer inside and touch the magical thing. Then the helicopter's blades began to whir; clouds of dust once more billowed up; the bird rose and left as it had come, across the tops of the guava and eucalyptus trees its blades thumping, above Sho and Fungom, across the fields of Kikfuini and Baingo, growing smaller until, no more than a dot, it disappeared through the cleft between the same two hills whence it had come. We waited for the dust to settle. The people who had come to watch began to drift away. We students made our way back to our classes. I believe that everybody who witnessed the arrival of the helicopter felt that the show had more than met their expectations, and have no doubt that every one of them retains an image of that day that is just as clear as mine.

Back in school, none of us could concentrate on our studies. Even the teachers had been amazed by the event and seemed as stunned as us. For weeks afterward the helicopter was discussed in all of its particulars by everyone I knew, each of us sharing our points of view and the emotions which the thing had stirred in us. The noise of the thing persisted, physically at first, so that my ears were ringing for a day or more, and after that just as loudly in my imagination. This noise was far greater than any I had ever known, incredible, beyond my powers of comprehension even though I'd witnessed it myself. For weeks, for months, for years I heard the helicopter's whirring blades, as, too, I hear them even now.

The event confirmed our good opinions of a people who could not only create such a thing as this helicopter but who might honor our leaders with a ride in one. Americans, after all, brought us besides miraculous machines clean water and free medicines. They brought us books to read and school supplies. They brought us the idea of democratic institutions—an idea which, I'm hard-pressed to understand, we were taught in school. It seems strange to me that we who lived in a country that was run then, as it is now, by a dictator, were allowed to learn the virtues of an institution that is anathema to the man. But we were.

So too as we learned that America was the greatest democracy in the world, did we understand from everyday experience that Americans were uniformly honest, fair, egalitarian. I knew this firsthand because of the way I was treated by the midwives at our Maternity Center. In my country there was little of egalitarianism and even less of honesty in government. One was born to one's rung on the ladder of life, which was nearly impossible to climb. As I knew so well, one could not rise above his station without a helping hand adept at greasing palms, reaching down to lift one up. One must be ambitious to succeed, but ambition alone could never be enough. Indeed, I knew a great number of bright, ambitious girls and boys whose parents were too poor to send them to primary school; primary school graduates who could not afford secondary school. So on up the ladder: fewer still could afford a high school education; only the rich could send a child to university.

In America, it seemed to me, things surely must be different.

I made my closest observations of Americans and their relations with the Kom in Bobe David's and Nawain Martha's house. David Cheng, as an important figure in our village, had occasion to entertain the Americans who were working on the Belo Water Project—an enterprise conceived by the government of Cameroon to bring fresh water from the mountain village of Anyajua to the other villages of Kom. Each village was responsible for completing the miles of trenches that ran within its borders with vol-

unteers recruited for the purpose. Hundreds of hours of labor
were required, so that every week each Village Head would mobi-
lize his villagers as a general raises an army, to swing the picks and
spades required to do the job. I myself volunteered my time to
work on the project, and recall the pride that we all felt at accom-
plishing the task.

Of the engineers who oversaw this project, though—the white
Americans in other words—I remained as terrified as I was fascinated. I served them at Bobe David's table, and while they ate I
peeked at them from behind closed doors. That they were other-
worldly was confirmed to me by the sight of their eating fufu corn
with forks instead of fingers. David, I could see, was taken absolutely as their equal. They could not have seen me watching them.
They could not have known how intensely I studied them as I
retrieved their empty dishes, or how much influence they were
having on my life merely by treating Bobe David as they treated
one another. Nor could they have known how much their presence, like the arrival of the helicopter, strengthened my resolve to
leave the place behind.

In all the years I spent at Bobe David's house, though, and no
matter how much I yearned to find a better world, I never ceased
to care for those whom I had left behind in Fungom, or to miss the
mother who had given me the opportunity to dream of something
else. I visited my mom once a year and she visited me at school
once or twice a year. It was with the greatest joy that at school
holidays I found my mother at our door. She walked from Fungom
bearing gifts of yams or beans, without agenda other than to chat
with me. She came. She stayed an hour over tea. We traded news
of this and that. How were my siblings? How was Uncle Seing?
What of Uncle Diffrey? Of Nawain and Victorine? Mother's visits
seemed to please even Martha, whose mood always brightened
and whose attitude towards me grew kind. For these reasons I

recall my mother's visits only warmly, with a smile. Her presence, her own joy in seeing me, the pride she had in my accomplishments—all these renewed my determination to justify her faith in me.

One day, though, Mother 's arrival gave us cause for alarm. The strangeness of the hour alone was enough to have provoked concern, for though night had not yet fallen, the sun had set and the sky shown in the darkest hue of blue. As alarming as the hour was the fact that she was not alone, for she carried on her back my brother Samuel, a sweet boy two years my junior who suffered from mild learning disabilities. He had always been a sickly child. We knew somehow that he did not have long to live, as indeed, he didn't: Samuel would die of unknown causes two years later. Among his afflictions Samuel had been born with cracked and swollen feet, a condition that had persisted throughout his life and made walking difficult. My mother carried Samuel everywhere.

On seeing the two of them standing at the door, even Martha expressed a genuine concern, which I had not seen in her before.

That morning as my mother explained, Samuel had begun to fuss. She soon determined that the child had managed to lodge in his nose a white plastic button, which she had attempted to remove. She tried with no success every method she could conceive to pull the button out, and, in time, she resolved to seek treatment in Belo. By the time she left Fungom the late-afternoon shadow of Bobong hill had overspread the village. For an hour or more, up and down the trails I knew so well, she carried Samuel through Fungom, Sho, and Kichu. And when, at dusk, she reached the Maternity Center in Belo, she found the midwives there equally unequipped to remove the button from my brother's nose. Samuel was whimpering; my mother was at her wit's end. The midwives explained that she had no choice but to carry the little boy to the hospital in Mbingo, ten miles to the west.

My mother despaired, for she must now contemplate such a journey along a hilly road at night, carrying a child who had begun to wheeze. The midwives inquired whether she had family in Belo. My mother had explained my presence there. In this way she resolved to come to us, so that I might help her on the way.

I remember the moment very clearly when I saw my mother standing at our door with Samuel on her back, an expression on her face of the most placid resolve, as though she were contemplating how many cocoyams she would need to pound that day for supper. I remember, too, just as clearly as my mother's face, the humanity that Nawain Martha showed—as if, having reached the brink of human disregard, she had found some love in her. Bobe David said at once that I must accompany my mother to the hospital—to translate her Kom into the English of the doctors, and then to put their words to Kom—and went to fetch a flashlight and a little money to carry with us. Martha for a time also disappeared, and, when she returned, she handed my mother a bottle of water for our trip, and a bag filled with bread and fruit.

Belo had grown dark by the time we three set out, only the lanterns in the houses flickering here and there. The road to Mbingo was darker still, and no less difficult to walk than my mother had imagined. Uphill and down we trudged, from time to time exchanging the burden of Samuel on our backs. His breathing grew worse. We took the shortest course, which frequently involved our finding shortcuts in the pitch-black night, stumbling over rocks, stepping into unseen holes, banging up against the brush that lined these little trails. In time, around 10:00 or so, we saw at last lights of Mbingo's village center, and, soon enough, the medical center itself.

The Mbingo Baptist Hospital consisted of three buildings connected by breezeways, and a separate house—luxurious by the standards of my country, made of stone with stucco walls—for the

American doctors who worked there. As far as I knew the hospital never closed. At the front desk someone took our names. Another person listened to the problem we described. In a short time we were escorted to a tiny room such as could scarcely have held two people and a couple of small goats, though I supposed that there was room for a doctor to squeeze in. I recall very clearly that the walls of this room were cracked, and that the concrete floor felt cool on my bare feet. There were no chairs in the room, or any other place to sit. We were exhausted. I watched Samuel sleeping fitfully in Mother's arms.

Not long after we arrived I heard the sound of someone entering our room.

"Good evening!" said a voice.

I trembled at the sound of it.

And when I turned I saw that a white man in an even whiter lab coat—the doctor, certainly—was reaching out to shake my hand. I was uncertain what to do, for though I had seen white people at the Belo Maternity Center and served dinner to Bobe David's guests, it had never occurred to me that I might touch one of them.

"I'm pleased to meet you," said the man.

At last I found my courage, and, reaching out myself, I shook the hand of Jesus.

This hand was the smoothest I had ever felt, or could ever have imagined. But though the experience was a novel one, the smoothness merely confirmed to me what I had always known: that white people were rich beyond imagination, unbearably happy, without want.

The experience changed my life, for I believed at that moment not merely that I was in the hands of Jesus, but that God Himself must be nearby. The shortness of my breath, the beating of my heart and the ringing of my ears, a sense of warmth overflooding me—all confirmed to me the facts of these divine presences. Every observation, every thought that I had ever had about Americans—about the things they made and the ideas they'd conceived—these were processed through the lens of this experience. Though my faith continues, and though I know that the doctor was no god, still the experience remains to me a highly religious one. It confirmed for me the desperate pull of America. It increased my desire to succeed. Like all epiphanies, it gave me to see the world from a perspective that I had not imagined to exist.

The doctor with a strange instrument, a sort of rod something like a long pair of tweezers attached to a little light, reached into Samuel's nose and within seconds pulled the button out.

My mother, Samuel, and I were equally astonished that so exhausting a walk had been required to accomplish such a simple task.

The doctor tossed the button into a metal bowl and asked my mother if there was anything else that he could do for her.

I translated.

My mother shook her head and thanked the man.

"Well then," said the doctor, "this will cost you 150 francs."

I blinked.

"I don't have that much, sir," I told the man.

"You don't?" He asked. "How much do you have? You do have money, don't you?"

"Yes, sir. I have 50 francs."

The doctor thought a moment and smiled.

"Very well," he said. "This will cost you 50 francs."

The doctor told me how proud I ought to be of caring for my mother and my brother as I had, and what a pleasure it had been to help us.

When he had left, the nurses gave us the button as a keepsake.

We ate our fruit and bread, and went to sleep on a bed of banana leaves in the overcrowded guest house that served the patients' visiting relatives.

CHAPTER EIGHT

Once a year or so, when Pa Andrew and his family turned up by car to vacation at a house they owned nearby, they would visit us in Belo. From my first meeting of the man, and on every one thereafter, I watched him with the fearful awe and unbounded hope of the supplicant.

He seemed to take his obligation seriously and was always kind to me. He would pat me on the head, inquire of my progress in school, and repeat what he had told me earlier: if I studied hard, I might go to live with him in Buea. From these meetings I took away the resolution to work harder for his sister, without complaint, as if on my knees just as my mother had advised.

If Martha asked me to scrub the floor, though I had done it yesterday, I scrubbed the floor from wall to wall. I prepared the meals with care to avoid any mistakes for which she had admonished me, in the hope not that she would praise me to Pa Andrew, but that she would complain less of me. Of the duties that she gave me there was one, though, that I thought might at least a little advance my cause with her important brother. Several times a year Martha sent me to help their aged parents in Njinikejem, which lay three miles away and up yet another tedious hill.

The parents were always grateful for my help. I performed small chores around their house; I helped them clear their land and harvest coffee beans—all in the most cheerful spirit I could summon—and used the good manners that my mother had impressed on me so that the Ndonyis might commend my character and hard work. The father owned a coffee farm atop the steep Njinikejem hill. Pa himself owned another one in Njinikejem as well as a vacation home he kept there. He seemed always to be adding rooms to the house, and I also helped with their construction—digging foundations, mixing cement, hauling bricks and stones and water to the site—all with an eye to the light in which my labor might be cast.

My hard work and humble manner did pay off, for during my last year in the Belo school Pa Andrew told me at last that he would take me that summer to live with him in Buea. He set one condition: that before he sent me to the middle school in Mamfe I would work for a while as a servant for his family. I suppose he wanted to know me first-hand before using his connections to place me in the school. But I had no fear of failing in the task of serving them. I had had a great deal of practice at the job.

That summer, a week or so before Pa was expected to arrive and I to go away, I walked to Fungom to tell my family and my friends goodbye. I saw my Uncle Seing; I saw Uncle Diffrey; I walked to Anjang to see my nominal father, Barnabas Afuma, and visited with extended family in Bobong and Anjin. With the men I shared a meal and drank the palm wine that is a tradition with Kom at leave-takings. My mother made me a dinner of fufu. My sisters gathered around, proud of me and my accomplishments, supportive of my future. My siblings regarded me as a father in something of the way that my mother considered me her husband—with all the rights of that paternal figure, but all the obligations too. My mother was overjoyed at the news that all her sacrifice had paid off. We too shared a cup of wine. She loved me, she said. She would always love me. Once more she counseled hard work and humility. I should expect to be treated badly, for that was the way of life. I should be kind to those I met on my way up the ladder; they were the same people that I would meet on my way back down again.

She held my hands, palms up, and spit on each of them.

"Ayeah," she said to me as she pressed my hands together.

She always called me Ayeah with affection and the deepest sense of love.

"This is my strength," she said. "This is my power from my ancestors to you. Whenever you step on a rock, only the rock will break."

She cried a little and waved to me as I walked away. She knew, I think, that the boy who was leaving now was leaving forever; that when her son returned he would be very different from the one she'd sent away.

Pa Andrew when he arrived in Belo with his family told me to prepare for the twelve-hour trip to Buea that lay ahead. We would be leaving on Saturday morning and carrying with us some supplies. I was nearly sick with the anticipation of this journey. Not once had I been inside a car of any kind, or traveled further than the four-hour walk that I had sometimes made to Abuh. Buea lay on the coast to the west of us, more than 200 miles away. On the appointed day, with what few possessions I'd acquired, I climbed into Pa's Land Rover with his wife and children, whom I knew from past visits.

I was afraid as I recall, but thrilled too by the sound of the engine and the smell of the exhaust mixing with the dust of the road. Friends and acquaintances stood around to see me off, and I remember thinking how odd it was that though a few of them waved goodbye to me, most stood silently and without expression, merely staring at the boy from Fungom who was leaving them behind. I have little doubt that my friends were happy for me, but there was too, as I see now, something of a sadness in those stares at watching me go. My good fortune could not have helped but to remind them that they, having no connections such as I, would never make the journey to a distant place and to the sort of future that awaited me.

The trip was long, hot, dusty, yet I never tired. For me the most eventful moments were those in which we were stopped by gendarmes dressed in khaki, their hands out to collect what might have been generously described as tolls. Pa Andrew had told me of these men, explaining that he was to do all the talking and that if the authorities questioned me I should answer honestly. But if I was hoping for some argument from the gendarmes, I was disappointed. The Rover bore government plates, because of which we were always waved through without ceremony.

I had no notion of the city to which we were headed. In fact, Buea is a quite exotic place. It sits by the sea on the slopes of Mt. Cameroon, a stunningly beautiful volcano which, at 13,000 feet, is the tallest mountain in West Africa. The town had been the capital of the German colony of Kamerun, and still retains in the palace of the governor—a lovely structure built by an opulent industrialist—a flavor of grand colonialism as imagined by the Germans. I would come to remember Buea as cool, humid, and rainy, with fog always hanging in the roads.

We arrived in the early evening when the streetlights had come on, and I remember staring in wonder not just at the lamps, but at all the wires required to light them. The streets were wider here, the cars more numerous, the houses larger than any I had seen before. The salty odors of the ocean reached out across the city, giving it an even more exotic air, for I had never smelled the sea.

People walked about in great numbers, dressed in the sort of clothes that we in Belo saved for Sundays and wearing sweaters against the chill.

In Belo I had tried to imagine what Pa's house might be like. Friends and neighbors had attempted to explain the concept of electricity, but to me who had seen only one bulb lit by it, the stuff remained a mystery. The telephone they had described as something that allowed one to talk to others far away. But how? On what principle could such a thing be possible? I was told that the houses in places like Buea possessed indoor kitchens, where water ran day and night at a tap like the one that stood outside our Maternity Center. But I could not conceive of how that might really be.

Pa's house when I first laid eyes on it more than met my expectations. It was a sprawling, single-story affair, painted white and topped by a hipped roof. I thought it huge. A fence surrounded it; a wide porch fronted it; a guest house stood next door. In lovely gardens surrounding it Christ-thorn and other flowers bloomed.

The guest house served relations of the Ndonyis who passed through town for days or months or years. These included a step-brother, Benjamin, with whom I had worked in Njinikejem, and Pa Andrew's oldest son, Victor, with whom I would share a room.

Inside the main house I was shown about the place. Here was the parlor-dining room. Here was the kitchen, where, as promised, water ran at one's command. Here were the bathrooms—two of them. Here were four bedrooms—one for Ma and Pa and the others divided among their eight children, who to me seemed utterly sophisticated. For two or three days I walked about in a fog. Each new appliance required some time even to conceive. In the kitchen, a stove lit by bottled gas could be turned on and off at will. A refrigerator, humming, kept food from spoiling. A freezer held ice—theretofore known to me only in the form of hail—

which sat side by side with frozen meats. The use and operation of
the toilets was explained, but for some time I feared that beneath
my hand harm would come to them.

By far the most amazing instrument encountered in Pa's house
was the telephone of which in Belo I'd been warned, and which
sat on a table in the parlor. It was by today's standards quite old-
fashioned. It's ring was loud. The first time someone called I
jumped, startled, and turned to see what could be making such a
sound. Within a day or so, after I had watched the other children
racing to answer it, I wished to answer the telephone as well. In
time it rang. I lifted the receiver. A voice at the other end, in the
accent that only white men used, inquired if Mr. Ndonyi was at
home. Yes! I thought. He was! And I would go and fetch him! And
then, believing that the phone's cradle was the receiver's proper
place, I promptly hung it up. Pa's children laughed at that, and
explained my mistake. From that moment forward, I never failed
to race Victor and his siblings in the game of getting to it first.

My chores in Buea were of the light household kind, for there
was no farm to cultivate, no wood to chop, no corn to grind or
cocoyams to pound. I cooked. I cleaned. I raked the yard and
weeded flower beds. With Mama Theresia I bought groceries at
the market. In the backyard I ran water into buckets with a hose—
this, a novelty as well—and washed the family's clothes and hung
them on a line and, when they were dry, ironed them carefully. I
also served Pa Andrew, who like Bobe David, was fastidious. His
shoes must be shined just so. His breakfasts—of fried eggs and
fried plantains and the fried potatoes we called *dodo*, and oatmeal,
grapefruit, tea—must be made just the way he liked them. When
he was finished his plates must be quickly cleared away.

Of all the jobs I had during my stay in Buea, the one that I
enjoyed most was helping Mama run a so-called "off-license" establishment she owned, where people bought Beaufort, Gold

Harp, and other beers, and Top Citron and Fanta soda pop. Some customers drank at the tables that were scattered there, some carried their liquids home, while I made change and kept strict accounts. Mama's other children were never employed in the off-license store. I believe she felt that Victor and the others would not be as careful as I.

In contrast to my time in Belo, the days I spent in Buea were comfortable. I had leisure time, which I had not had under Nawain Martha's eye. The family was kind to me. Pa Andrew seemed to be a just, fair man. Mama was warm and loving. Though I was a country boy, they and Victor and the others were patient of my mistakes in learning all their city ways, never laughing meanly at my ignorance.

But though the experience was a vast improvement over my previous life, I could not help feeling an outsider as I had felt since leaving home, a servant rather than a member of the family. Like Emmanuel, Victor performed light chores, but though he might help me with mine, it was I who was responsible. Nor was Mama Theresia entirely unforgiving. She sometimes sent unsubtle messages on the competence of my work, flooding the floors with water for example, to hint that they must be better washed.

The family, in other words, saw me as someone who belonged in the place from which he'd come. They expected me to stay there, serving them unseen, while they gathered in the living room. It seemed to me that they believed they were better folks than I; and that, though the thought was never spoken, they considered me an orphan and a bastard who deserved his lot in life. I was no stranger to such treatment: I'd known it ever since I moved to Belo, and lived with Nawain Martha for a while. Still, I had thought that Pa and Mama and the rest would be above such prejudice.

Day in and day out, month after month, I was haunted by the fear, no less constant than the fear I'd had in Belo, that my work was a sort of down payment for my education—a payment in coin whose value had not been firmly set. Not only must my duties be performed well enough today—the shine as it should be; the creases in the dress, the trimming of the hedges, the frying of the eggs just so—but it must be good enough in what might be the harsher light shone on it tomorrow. How can one know without some reassurance that one's work is good enough?

A memoir is no objective accounting: we select our memories, after all, because they're essential to our self-regard. Pa Andrew, Mama Theresia, Victor and the rest surely have different memories of the time I spent in Buea. To them, I might have seemed not quite so hardworking as I recall. To them I might have been as much a burden to feed, to clothe, to house as I was a help in serving them. Still, objectivity is sometimes overrated: though Nawain Martha no doubt recalls my work in Belo as a great deal less than adequate, I'm certain she is wrong.

CHAPTER NINE

Successful men like Pa Andrew—managers, negotiators, businessmen—have an ability to separate goals from human feelings. In a sense I was for Pa the good that lay in the middle of a transaction: he owed a debt to Maiyili's family for Maiyili's having schooled him; I was a member of Maiyili's family; he therefore was responsible for schooling me. As it happened though, I was a good not quite equal to that which he had been: I had been born out of wedlock and was, officially at least, an orphan. He therefore felt justified I imagine in extracting from me a year's labor, which I guess he'd figured as the difference.

Of successful men, however, there are two types: those who use every means possible to escape their debts and those like Pa Andrew who, though they might figure a charge otherwise than some, will pay it nonetheless. Pa was an honorable man, and when a year was up he undertook to settle what he owed. I was seventeen I think when he carried me to the little town of Mamfe, a six-hour drive north of Buea and near the border with Nigeria, where he intended to enroll me in the St. John's Technical Commercial College (for "college" in Cameroon is another word for secondary school, and both are used for what Americans would call middle school). In town he took me shopping for the school uniform of khaki shorts and yellow shirts and sandals, as well as the other clothes I'd need. It was then that I received the first pair of leather shoes I'd ever owned, from which I derived, as I believed, a look of cultivation.

St. John's when Pa and I rolled up exceeded my expectations. The school sat in the middle of a hundred acres of woods and fields where the locals went to hunt, farm, and fetch wood. The campus itself was something like a half-mile square and required ten minutes to walk from one end to the other. Two long buildings of classrooms formed the center of the place. Behind these lay a large dormitory which housed the girls. A Catholic church stood at one end. Houses for the Reverend Father and several of the teachers were scattered here and there. A grass soccer field, a volleyball court, a separate building for the cafeteria all gave me to feel that I was, if not quite rich, then certainly well-off. This feeling was enhanced by the reception I received on arriving with Pa Andrew in his car. Few of the students' families owned cars. My prospective schoolmates formed immediately the impression that I came from a family of wealth. And though I did not encourage my friends in this view, neither did I do much in the ensuing years to dispel the misconception.

When my enrollment was complete, Pa took me to the home of a former employee of his with whose family I'd live. Their house was a fine brick structure—among the nicest in the village of Nsang, close-by to Mamfe, where St. John's was located. The family for the next four years would be very kind to me, without the least intention as I had feared of monitoring my whereabouts. I would share two rooms with James, a relation of theirs who, though my age, was worldlier than I. He supported himself as a trader at the Mamfe market from biking across the border to buy clothes, and from tapping palm trees in the jungle, whose sap he used to make palm wine. The patriarch of the family was to be, as I soon learned, more problematic—an alcoholic, often drunk, who though warm and affectionate when sober was when in his cups volatile and mean, talking nonsense that unnerved me.

When Pa had seen to my settling-in, we said our goodbyes. If he had not been as kind to me as my Uncles Seing and Diffrey and Bobe David were, if he thought I was not quite his equal, still he seemed proud of my accomplishments and happy to be sending a boy on his way to something better than a life of tending goats and pulling weeds. We parted on good terms, I thankful and he gracious, without the air of self-congratulation that many in his place might have shown.

What can one say of one's first real independence? Next to love it must be among the greatest feelings in the world to live more or less as one chooses, to have a little money to rattle in one's pocket, and to enjoy one's free time without the shadow of a parent or guardian watching over him. The girls were made to live on campus. For the boys, though—especially those like me whose families did not live nearby—our time spent outside school was our own. How wonderful it was! I reveled in my freedom like a canary loosed from its cage, and could hardly know—as no one can who first sets out on his own—how profoundly the experience would change me.

Mamfe was as different from Buea as Buea had been from Belo, and if there were in the town few new technologies to wonder at, still every moment I spent there brought the joy of new experience. Where Buea had been filled with the breezes of the ocean, and Belo, like Fungom, with cool mountain airs, Mamfe was hot, humid, wet. More than 100 inches of rain fall there each year, which during the summer months comes down in torrents, ceaselessly. Jungle surrounds the town, where elephants, tigers, and hippopotamuses are to be found, and even, in the enormous game preserves that begin 20 miles to the north and east, gorillas.

Though Mamfe when I was there was a small place of dirt roads and dilapidated buildings, where one ran not infrequently into men dressed in loincloths, its proximity to Nigeria gave the town something of an international air: unlike James, most of the traders at the market were Nigerians who came across the border every week to sell their wares. Something of the town's past as an outpost of the German empire remains in a tower—the area's chief attraction—that is occupied by the senior divisional commander—as well as in the town's main road which was paved before, and has not been much repaired since, 1914.

A river, the Manyu, flows past Mamfe. In the rainy season this river is muddy, swift, and dangerous, stretching a hundred yards from bank to sandy bank. Besides the divisional commander's tower, the area's other attraction is a bridge across the river that was built by the Germans in 1904—made of rope, planked, suspended from two pretty concrete towers—which, during the rainy season, the jungle nearly overtakes. When I was there, the chief means of communication across the Manyu and through the jungle thickets was by drumming. In contrast to these surroundings, St. John's College seemed quite civilized to me.

At St. John's a strict discipline was maintained. The principal was a sister of sixty years or more, ugly as I then considered her, with a long nose and a stooped walk that made her waddle like a duck. Her name was Sister Declean. I'm ashamed to recall how we snickered at the woman behind her back—quacking like ducks and flapping our arms and, like all the villagers, calling her "Maagbor." I'm not sure I ever knew what Maagbor meant, but I know she didn't like it.

Sister Declean never wavered in her insistence on obedience. Corporal punishment was not inflicted at the school, but if we skipped our classes we were made to carry firewood from the forest or to cut the grass with cutlasses. We liked to lie among the bushes of an overgrown pineapple farm that stood a mile away, eating the ripe fruit, and, when we were sated, taking some home with us. If we were caught at this activity when we should have been in school, as of course we sometimes were, we were similarly punished.

The faculty of St. John's were mostly Cameroonians. In my first year one white teacher had a place on the college faculty; in the next year two more joined. These white women had come as missionaries from Ireland, a place that for some time I imagined as a region of America. They entranced me. On one of them—Miss Murphy, a sweet, curly-haired beauty—I formed a crush that lasted years. Among other courses, Miss Murphy taught typing, a skill at which she herself excelled. She could produce 80 words or more a minute without mistake, on the manual typewriters that were to me wondrous inventions. My memory grows sharp when I recall myself watching Miss Murphy type. Time slows. I can see her fingers flashing here and there across the keys, and feel the awe that her powers filled me with. I recall too the affection that she seemed to have for me alone, even as she concentrated on the task at hand. From Miss Murphy I myself learned to type nearly 70 words in 60 seconds.

I recall my other studies vividly as well: the classes in religion, which we uniformly loathed; in history—of the Enlightenment, of the slave trade, of colonial rule; in reading, writing, and geography. We took French as well, though curiously, for a country whose majority population speaks that language, we did not gain a fluency in it. My favorite classes were in literature. We read the Greek plays and Shakespeare—*Macbeth* and *Julius Caesar* I espe-

cially recall—and Achebe, Orwell, Austen. I was astonished to
discover on reading *Pride and Prejudice* that the theme which my
mother had so drilled into me was a universal one. Pride, I knew,
was among the deadly sins, but it had not occurred to me that
white people too might stoop beneath its burden.

As wonderful as the opening of a world which had not theretofore existed was the freedom that came of living on my own. Owing to the pocket money given to me by Pa Andrew, or sent to me
by David Cheng or Mother, I was, though by no means the most
affluent of the students, rich beyond anything I'd known. With my
newfound wealth I ventured forth with friends—Bakor Roy, Elias
Ekwa, Rose Ebang, Helen Nojang—to Mamfe, where we dined at
any number of its little restaurants or browsed among its shops. I
quickly learned the fashions of our school. I bought bellbottoms
and plaid dress shirts, which I'd leave unbuttoned to the navel,
and t-shirts bearing images of John Travolta and Michael Jackson.

Elias Ekwa was, besides being one of my best friends, the
school's star soccer player, whose popularity lent cachet to me.
Elias lived in a mud house roofed with palm fronds, which he
rented with some other boys at the school. I and others would
meet there to sip a cup of wine (a locally distilled sweet milky wine
of the palm) and chat. Some who came even enjoyed Elias's cooking, though I never ate with him. He lived across the way from the
restaurateur whose menu offered dog meat, and though Elias
himself never touched dog, I couldn't bring myself to eat even that
food which had been cooked in the same pots and pans.

Among the activities I liked best were the events that were
jointly organized with the Queen of Rosary School, a girls' acade-
my in nearby Okoyond whose Irish missionary teachers were
friends of our instructors. We were carried by soldiers in army
trucks to watch the plays of Shakespeare put on by the girls of
QRS; they came to disco dances that we put on in the cafeteria,

complete with mirrored globes, where we hopped about to the sounds of the saxophones, the synthesizers, the pianos, guitars, and snare drums of makossa—a funky dance genre with roots in jazz and Latin music.

The heights of our weeks were the soccer matches that we played on a field in Mamfe against other area schools. The army trucks collected us—the boys as the heroes and the girls to cheer us on.

My friend Elias was the team's captain, its fastest player, its best scorer and defender, who played as well on a team in town. The games were quite unlike those played by middle-schoolers in America. Fistfights broke out on the issues of calls, when spectators spilled onto the field and melees ensued. The fights, however ferocious, were in good fun, and at the end of the games we palled around with our opponents. Afterwards we rode home in the dark, exhausted but exhilarated, the girls and boys jostling against each other, when, sometimes, ecstatically, our arms chanced to rub together.

I was not a brawler. During our soccer matches I stood at the fringes of the crowd, watching the flinging fists and cheering on my team, but rarely participating. At school as well I avoided conflict. I fought only once as I remember with not a little shame, but with the knowledge too that sometimes one must fight to avoid the humiliation that comes of letting others take advantage. There was at the school a bully named Anyere—the sort of troubled youth who is always picking fights. He tormented the smaller children and had, on more than one occasion, given me a shove or trod upon my toes. One day though, when our class was clearing the pineapple farm of its grass and other overgrowth, Anyere punched me in the face.

The blow startled me at first, for it had come without provocation or other obvious cause. A rage filled me that I'd never felt before. I cast about for a weapon, and, finding large, heavy tree branch lying on the ground, I picked it up and swung it at Anyere's head with all the force at my disposal. I was full-grown by then, well-built and strong from my labor in the fields of Kom. Anyere dropped without a sound and lay motionless at my feet. I thought I'd killed the boy. The teachers and the other children were as shocked as I—not just from the sight of the school bully lying still upon the earth, but from having witnessed such brutality in one so ordinarily pacific as I. Anyere was carried to the Mamfe hospital, where the doctors diagnosed a concussion from which he'd soon recover. I went the next day to my classmate's house to apologize for hitting him, and offered to pay for the expenses that his family had incurred in treating him. But Anyere declined my offer and admitted that he'd started the fight. I should add that despite the scare that this occasion gave me, Anyere never bothered me again.

At Christmas and summer holidays everyone departed to make their separate ways towards home. On these occasions Pa Andrew would send a driver to collect me, so that once again my mates waved goodbye to him who seemed their wealthy friend. These trips were not always pleasant. I was nearly killed once when my driver on a sharply winding curve flipped Pa's Land Rover into a ditch. I remember lying on my back staring at the sky and listening to the driver's agony. He died, I think, in the hospital where we were carried.

For the most part, though, I felt like a dignitary as I was chauffeured to Mamfe and back. I thought it ironic that I should be viewed at school as the scion of a fortune, when, on my homecoming to Buea, I returned to the servitude that was my lot with the Ndonyis. I remember fondly the Christmas stews of chicken and rice that Mama Theresia would prepare, but I remember as well how perplexing it was to reconcile my status at the school with my standing in their home. In Mamfe I could forget how dependent was my plight on the caprice of human nature. In Buea, my station was made plain again.

The long summer breaks, when I returned to Kom, were altogether different from my holiday sojourns with Pa and his family. The trips themselves were more exhausting. In the place of Pa's fancy car I was forced either to take public transportation—standing, cheek by jowl with scores of others for hours without a break—or to ride in the beds of pickup trucks for miles along the country's unpaved roads. I'd arrive in Belo covered in the dust that billowed up—a powder so white, so fine, so completely obscuring of the skin that lay beneath, that a friend once compared me to a ghost.

I found on my return to Belo that Nawain Martha did not treat me as ill as formerly. Though she held me in no greater esteem than she had when I'd left home, she knew that the rest of the community looked up to me as a scholar and treated me as something of a celebrity. I could read and write now better than most people in the village, and spoke English fluently. I wore the latest fashions—the bellbottoms, the leather shoes, the rakishly unbuttoned shirts—and carried an air of refinement and maturity that I'd lacked two years before.

Among the skills that led to my new standing in the village were my talents for writing and translation. Returning students such as I became the scribes of the community, whom friends, relatives, and neighbors often asked to write their letters. As Kom is not even now a written language, I put their words into English for a scribe at the other end to translate into the original. These requests came most often from women whose husbands were working the coastal plantations, soliciting money for example to defray the costs of pregnancies and births. I was proud of my skills and touched by the nearly universal expressions of love, often poetically expressed, that filled these missives.

My writing during holidays came in handy at home as well. David by then had grown nearly deaf, though no less concerned with world affairs, and asked if I would listen to the news on his shortwave radio and transcribe it for him as best I could. I was happy to oblige, and got so good at it that he told me I ought to become a journalist. In this way, too, I translated onto the written page the words spoken by those who came to call on him—either that, or repeated word for word everything they said by shouting in his ear.

The long vacations were filled mostly with the work required to produce from the fertile fields of Kom sustenance for winter. Besides my chores for Nawain Martha—cutting grass and gathering the ripened vegetables; working on Pa's house in Njinikejem—one of the clearest memories I have of my first summer home is one I can't recall without a smile. It happened at the Maternity Center one day as I was fetching firewood that an older girl I vaguely knew lured me into a nearby outhouse. Though untutored in the ways of well-developed country girls, I followed her without question into the awful place. She had learned from experience that the toilet alone, of the places she could imagine, afforded any privacy, while I had no experience at all with such acts as might require it. In fact I hardly knew that I'd had sex by the time this girl had buttoned up her dress and left me there alone, puzzled by the strange event but nonetheless exhilarated. In time I must have understood what had taken place in the outhouse that day, for the next summer it occurred to me that I might ask the girl for more. When I found her, though, she flatly turned me down.

In this way through the seasons—from Buea to school and back again on holidays; from school to Belo in the summer months and back to school in Mamfe—I lived what were the happiest years of my life since leaving Fungom at the age of ten. I loved the disco dances. I loved the soccer matches and rubbing shoulders with the girls as we bumped and swayed our way home. I remember fondly the celebration of our country's independence each year on the 20th of May, when students from area schools assembled in Mamfe to sing patriotic songs and watch traditional dances organized by the locals.

I changed greatly while I was there. I was growing up into a man. I had developed a realistic view of the world. From geography and history I had learned that one might travel to America by airplane or by boat, but could not swim there. I learned that not everyone in America was wealthy, that life there for most people was not as *The Cosby Show* depicted it. I learned that white people were not Jesus, and that they had the same sorts of wants and needs as I. I learned that in America, black people suffered no less from discrimination at the hands of whites than we English speakers in Cameroon suffered at the hands of the French.

CHAPTER TEN

In the months before my graduation from St. John's, Pa's Office of Community Development had been moved from Buea to Yaoundé—the nation's capital; the site of the country's most prestigious university; a city where a million people lived. It was there, then, that I moved when my years in secondary school were finished. To my little-traveled eyes the city was astonishing. I had never before seen the president's house—a gargantuan modernist structure of six stories—which I thought stunning. Embassies, government offices, businesses, and shops drew people past our new house in a fascinating stream. There were more cars in Yaoundé, more busses and sleek, late-model taxicabs, more white people than I had ever seen before. The city gave off an air of affluence that I had never imagined might exist in Cameroon.

My relationship to Pa Andrew's family did not change. As in Buea I shared a room with Victor. As in Buea I found comfort in the company of my cousin Benjamin, who, I found when I arrived, had moved there to enter university. As in Buea, I kept the house and served the family: no mention was made of *my* entry into high

school. As in Buea, each night I shined the shoes that Pa would
wear to work. I swept the floors and tidied up, made the beds,
shopped for groceries at the market.

On most weekdays Pa returned for lunch. He liked to bring
guests home with him—Cameroonians and other Africans, Europeans and Americans. He had a stereo and a great many records,
and liked to play for his visitors the American music of which he
was fond—Linda Ronstadt, I remember, and the Eagles. Mama
Theresia cooked while I waited on the table—the servant, invisible, not worth the trouble of noticing. Years later, in fact, when I
ran into people who had dined with us and mentioned that we'd
met, they would have no recollection at all of me.

Life otherwise was tolerable; I frequently enjoyed myself.
Among my fondest memories of those days in Yaoundé was watching the pretty girls who walked by our house to and from their
schools. There was one in particular—I never learned her name—
whom I thought exquisite, and who passed each day in uniform.
She lived down the street in a house that bore a wooden sign
painted with the words "Chien Méchant"—"Vicious Dog." Such
signs were common about the town. But though some referred to
vicious dogs, many, like the one that fronted this girl's house, had
been placed there by wary fathers to scare away their daughters'
suitors.

Such was life. The days turned into weeks, the weeks into
months, and still I awaited word of the schooling for which my
servitude was paying. I was still a shy country boy at heart and Pa
was an important man. One did not approach such men to ask
when they might make good their promises. And even when, after
I'd been a year in Yaoundé, and Pa mentioned that he would be
sending me to interview for a place in high school, my frustration
did not abate: I would be applying to the school, as he explained—
but not until another year had passed.

My eagerness to enter school, and thus to get on with my life, was matched by my frustration. Beyond the occasional conversation with Benjamin, I had no one in whom to confide. In a sense, as an outsider in the family and far away from home, I was, despite the companionship of Benjamin and Victor and the rest of the children, quite alone. My impatience rose like a flower from the earth, until in time it bloomed into resentment.

I had encountered much frustration in my life and had been without a confidante for years, and so had learned to express myself with pen and ink. Thus I sat down one day to put on paper all my many grievances. I vented my anger that I should be left home as a servant while the children went off to school each day. I cursed my illegitimacy. I lamented the fact that as an orphan I must suffer punishment for a crime in which I'd had no part.

Self-pity, I had found, often soothes the soul.

Who hasn't at one time or another felt the burden of frustration? Who hasn't resented life's unfairness? For unfairness is a state of mind, and life's unfair to everyone in small or greater ways.

I cried when I had finished writing.

One day, though—a day like any other, and so surprisingly—Pa came to me and said that he'd arranged for me to interview at St. Paul's, a well-known high school in a village near Buea. For my interview I'd be staying with a friend of his, the Reverend Yongkuma, with whom Pa had grown up. I myself knew the minister and his children well, for they had dined with us in Buea on more than one occasion. He was a serious but kindly man who wore black-rimmed glasses and had the habit—which we children found immensely funny—of taking on each visit the same corner of the sofa, and placing a side cushion beneath his arm in exactly the same way.

Pa seemed genuinely happy that I would at last be going to high school. And though he couldn't know the extent of my ecstasy, he appeared to understand how important the occasion was.

He placed a hand on my shoulder.

"I have the utmost confidence in you being accepted," he told me. "You did well in secondary school and will do well at St Paul's."

I thanked him and told him that I would work hard to make him proud of me.

In three or four weeks' time I took the bus to Buea, where the pastor collected me, and, in the morning had an interview with the principal of St. Paul's—a Catholic priest and friend of Pa's whose name I recall as Tubah.

The interview must have gone well. I heard some weeks later that I had been accepted and could now get on with the pursuit of my goals.

During the last days of summer, through their foggy nights and pleasant mornings and thunderstorms each afternoon, I grew more and more excited about the prospect of the new life to come. I began to pack several days before I was to leave, blissful, and hardly conscious of the present. A new home! New friends! Studies that would help me reach my dream, no less strong than it had been when I was ten, of going to America.

There was one thing, though, that gave me pause in my excitement, for I sensed a distancing of Pa's children from me for no reason I could imagine. In subtle and not so subtle ways they engaged in irrational, even bizarre behavior, whispering behind my back and falling quiet when I came into the room. There was nothing I could do about it though.

On the appointed day in the height of the rainy season, the roads a quagmire, I was packed like a sardine into a van with others of my species, and sent off to Buea. I remember nothing of the trip, for that and all the others that I've taken on public transportation in Cameroon run together in a way that wearies me even to consider them. I do recall my reception at the Reverend Yongkuma's, though, for I believe that my excitement was infectious. They were a warm family and seemed more than politely happy for my good fortune. And though I knew them from their visits to Buea, it struck me as soon as I walked in that I was being treated more as a member of their family than I had ever been since leaving Uncle Diffrey's house.

We ate dinner and sat about the living room to chat.

Later that evening the telephone rang.

It was Pa Andrew calling.

"*What*, Andrew?" the pastor said into the phone, in the sort of voice that could not express anything but shock.

I grew frightened, for the reverend's attitude was the sort that ensues from awful news that has not been adequately explained.

At last, he hung up the receiver and took a moment to consider what words to use with me.

"Pa Andrew wants you to go back to Yaoundé, Richard. He wants you to leave right away."

No one in the family stirred.

"But why?" I asked. "I don't understand!"

"He has changed his mind about you."

For a time no one spoke.

This was the sort of scene that witnesses do not forget. I was not merely stunned, for I would have felt the same sort of fear had Pa taken me aside to give the news in private. In front of strangers, though, I was humiliated. Not one of us could imagine what heinous act could have snatched a young man so abruptly from his dreams. The revelation of some awful secret? Theft, perhaps? Murder?

When we had taken in this news, the Reverend told us all that it was time to go to bed. In the morning, he explained, he would call a taxi to take me to the train station in Douala.

I couldn't sleep. I was twenty years old and yet I cried all night beneath my covers. I did not know how I could continue with my life. The end for which so much sacrifice was made had disappeared, and I could not imagine anything that might replace it.

"Why? Why?" I asked myself.

But no answer came to mind.

In the morning I went by taxi to Douala, where I was to return by train to Yaoundé. At the station when I had paid the driver and stepped out of the cab, I closed the door, expecting the driver to emerge to lift my suitcase from the trunk. Instead he drove away, and, for a minute, I could only watch his car growing smaller as it disappeared, doubtful of my senses. Had I really carried luggage with me? Did the taxi just depart with all of my possessions?

Soon enough I was confronted with the knowledge that the scene which seemed at first improbable had certainly occurred, that my suitcase was gone, and that I must try to find it.

But how?

Ought I to ask around?

Douala at the time was a city of nearly two million people. It is the center of the country's finance, media, and arts, and intimidating for any newcomer to the place. In Belo, in Buea, in Yaoundé one heard terrible stories of Douala, of killings, rapes, and robberies. What is more, unlike those familiar towns and cities the culture of Douala is entirely French. The signs are written universally in that language; the people to a man and woman have it as their native tongue; even those citizens who do speak English give the impression, doubtless passed on by our colonizers, of finding the task distasteful.

In my schoolboy French I inquired of passersby what I ought to do, and after some trouble was directed to the police station.

It dawned on me as I made my way that I would never make my train. Five minutes earlier I could not have imagined feeling any more despondent than I had been at hearing of Pa Andrew's inexplicable decision, and yet now on top of my shameful circumstance I must untangle the mess of a lost suitcase in a city of millions.

At the police station I was directed to an officer who not only spoke English, but did not mind using it. I will never forget the man. He listened to my story with a genuine concern and when, in time, he'd found my luggage, and determined that I had no place to stay, he asked me to come home with him.

He led me to his small apartment not far away, where he fed me. He listened to the longer version of my story.

"Richard," he told me when, exhausted, I had finished with my explanation, "the world is not always fair at first glance."

"No sir, not at all," I answered.

"There are things we can't explain and Lord knows I have seen many awful things in my days. Let me tell you though. If you are truly a good person inside and sincere in all you do, good seeks out good and we are protected by the energy within us, the energy that seeks out its own kind."

"Yes I agree," I said.

"I always wanted to be a police officer ever since I was a boy. I never wanted anything more out of life and am very content. I can see that you are a good person inside, but you are a wandering spirit. Your life appears to wind from here to there and at times you are met with hardships that are difficult for you. I'm glad that I was here to be able to help you and I know if given the same situation, you would also have helped me. It is who we are."

His house was small. There was no place for me to sleep except his bed, which he shared with me. In considering where else I might have spent that night I cannot imagine anyplace outside of Fungom—not Pa Andrew's house, certainly; not his sister's either—where I could have slept more peacefully than I did that night with a stranger in Douala. I was exhausted. Looking back I can see that my spirit was exhausted too, and required no less than my body and my mind the time to gather strength.

In the morning the policeman fed me breakfast and carried me to the station. We both knew that my train was heading to a place I didn't want to go, and that I had no choice in the matter. He turned away when we had parted company. We'd never meet again, I knew. And as I traveled east I could not help thinking of the man—his kindness, his generosity, his willingness to help a stranger with nothing except thanks given in return. I wondered then as I do now if angels really might exist, and whether, if they do, that policeman was among their number.

The trip took four hours. I had never ridden on a train before. The event would ordinarily have been one of anticipation and excitement. Now though, devastated, I could think of nothing but what was to me at that young age the greatest tragedy of my life. I slept most of the way, waking briefly as the train rattled through or stopped at one or another of the stations that we passed.

In Yaoundé when the cab had dropped me at Pa's house, Benjamin met me at the street and carried my luggage to the guest house where we roomed. He had in his possession a photocopy of the letter of complaint that I'd written to myself, and which, I guessed, one of the children had come upon. Benjamin told me it was a childish thing I'd done, which justified Pa's anger. And yet he was sympathetic to my plight, for he'd felt the same frustrations many times himself. In the room we shared he coached me on the approach I ought to take with Pa in explaining how I could have been so ungrateful for his help. I should lay myself at his feet in the most abject apology, with humility, deference, and perhaps even the expression of a little fear. The mood inside the house was tense. The children were afraid of their father when his mood grew dark; at dinner no one spoke.

When we had eaten Pa led me and Benjamin and Mama to the bedroom where my letter was produced. Pa handed it to me in order that I might refresh my memory and then in his commanding voice read the letter out loud to us. His fury frightened me. He was a man used to gratitude—that was how the system worked. One did favors in this world and expected loyalty in return. All this—however unfair I might think the punishment—was comprehensible to me. What I couldn't understand was that, as I soon saw, he blamed not me alone for my ingratitude, but my relatives as well. It was they, he said, who had planted the idea in me. It was they who were ungrateful. I suppose he understood that he'd been doing them as much a favor as he was doing me, and that the thanklessness of these adults was even worse than that of one so young as I.

In tears I pled my case—that I had merely wished to go to school; that the letter was a private sentiment not meant for other eyes; that I was more grateful than Pa could ever know for all that he had done for me. Could he not imagine my frustration at being left alone at home to scrub the floors while all the other children went to school? I begged him to forgive me. And as I pleaded for a second chance, Benjamin supported me. Yes, he said, it was a childish thing I'd done. Yes, I ought to be ashamed. Should such a letter though, however ill-advised, prevent me from going to high school?

But Pa was adamant and would not hear excuses. Though he had helped many people in the way that he'd been helping me, none of them had expressed such ingratitude as I. In his eyes such thanklessness meant that I did not accept him as a father. I read into his words the idea that he was done with me for good; that I was no longer a member of his family. He told me that in the morning he and Mama would carry me to Bamenda where my sister Angelina lived, and leave me there where I belonged.

To Bamenda we drove in silence. At Angelina's house I was greeted by the family with surprise and delight—the happy, warm, good humor that they felt at the unexpected visit of their celebrated relation—the boy who through the offices of an important man had escaped the dreary world in which they themselves were destined to remain. I'm sure my sister was puzzled at the sight of her brother's benefactor arriving without warning to produce me, luggage in hand, as if by magic from a lamp. We stood in the doorway watching Pa and Mama drive away, the Rover kicking up a cloud of dust that settled on our heads and clothes, on my suitcase, and, at last, on the floor around us.

CHAPTER ELEVEN

Had I a choice of all my siblings with whom to share a house, Angelina would, I think, have been the last. She is the second of my mother's children—a tall, thin, dark-skinned woman, brooding and temperamental—who had left home at an early age to marry and of whom I had only the vaguest memories. Her husband's name was Christopher Mdandam. He had come from a village nearby Fungom and was a policeman now. I hadn't seen either one of them in years.

From tiny Fungom Angelina had come up in the world. Besides her husband's income she made a living as a seamstress and knitter of sweaters. Her house, though without plumbing, had four rooms and a roof of tin, and was made partly of cement. Where Fungom had about 200 people, Bamenda at the time had something like 300,000, and was by far the largest city in the Grasslands. As the commercial center of a poor region in a third-world country, it was the sort of place that could afford to erect a few streetlights but not the power to run them every night. Its people came from nearby villages, whose tribes though related to the Kom spoke different languages. The lingua franca in Bamenda was a pidgin English.

It was dinnertime when Pa and Mama dropped me off at Angelina's house, and when the dust had settled we all sat down to eat. There remained for a while the air of excitement that had followed my arrival. I'd never seen the children. There were five of them, who to my happy surprise began at once to call me "Uncle." I was the relation who had been to school and was destined for great things. Angelina's husband Christopher warmly welcomed me as well, smiling, offering me dishes from the table, and asking after my health.

At last, though, my sister inquired to what they owed the pleasure of my company.

I told them as honestly as I was able, and as the family began to understand the import of my news, the sounds around the table hushed. For a moment everyone stopped eating. Even the smaller children, though they could not have said what had happened to their uncle, understood what it felt like to be disgraced in front of others: as I soon learned, they themselves faced humiliation daily in the presence of their mother. I cannot say if they wondered then whether punishment would follow my disgrace as it always followed theirs. My sister, though, received my news with compassion, and welcomed me to stay with them for as long as I needed.

In the days that followed, I discovered how profound is the exhaustion that comes of failure and dishonor. It seemed to me that my dreams had been crushed beneath Pa Andrew's shiny shoes. I could not imagine any future for myself. I languished for a while, moving slowly and sleeping much, helping out about the house like an automaton, deeply depressed, dissociated from my sibling, her family, the world. In time my spirits would improve. And yet looking back across the years I see that one never truly recovers from such shame and hopelessness, any more than one recovers from any other trauma.

From somewhere—I can't recall the source—I heard that Pa Andrew after dropping me at Angelina's house had driven on to Belo, where he gave the news of my faithlessness to Bobe David and Nawain Martha. One can only imagine how elated Martha was at the revelation of my failure. The news spread quickly. It wasn't long before my mother and my uncles had had it in bits and pieces, second-, third- and fourth-hand. From such reports I understood that my relations were furious at Pa, and that my mother, devastated, had sought the counsel of several witch doctors, paying each with a chicken for their troubles.

There was little for me to do in Bamenda. I knew no one. I had no job. My sister's neighborhood of dirt roads and small houses, though a step up from such primitive villages as Fungom, was a long way down the ladder of affluence that I had known in Buea and Yaoundé. Two secondary schools stood nearby, so that I could watch the girls walking back and forth between their houses. My sister, a Catholic, attended church at a nearby cathedral, where I joined her family for mass on Sundays. On occasion I went to soccer matches with Christopher, who was obsessed with the game in all its forms. Besides attending matches he played in a city league, and when not engaged in these activities he walked around with a shortwave radio pressed against his ear listening to broadcasts of the sport.

I felt sorry for the man, for as I quickly learned he was cowed by the sharp tongue of Angelina. She dominated him utterly. She nagged him constantly. She was opinionated, argumentative, and mercurial—often erupting from her quieter moods at the least offense from anyone around her. A tension filled the house morning, noon, and night, which at first I thought was caused by the addition of a large person into an already overcrowded home. I soon learned, though, that the tension was taken as a matter of course by everyone who lived there and that the atmosphere was a permanent condition. I hated it. I don't function well in tense and confrontational environments and soon enough was desperate to leave.

If Christopher suffered beneath my sister's scolding, the children fared worse. Besides the lashings from her tongue their missteps were met with ferocious slaps across the face while her husband quietly watched. She beat the children regularly and when they tried to run she grabbed them tightly by their arms and went at them once again. Even I who had grown up in a culture that accepted corporal punishment was horrified by her behavior, and felt unutterably sorry for the children. In time when I could no longer bear to watch, and began to express my sentiments to Angelina, she turned her rage on me.

It was a month before I began to feel myself again, and to recover my belief that however bleak the future seemed I would find my way through it. In proportion to my rising sprits my anger at Pa Andrew grew—an anger I don't think I had ever felt before except, perhaps, after the bully Anyere punched me in the face. From desperation to anger, from anger to rage I passed in measured steps, until, in time, my resolution grew to succeed in spite of him and in this way to prove him wrong.

When a month had passed I found the courage to make my way to Fungom, where at last I could tell my story unamended by Nawain Martha's exaggerations. My uncles were incensed by Pa's behavior, just as I had heard. My mother nearly cried. Her only solace until the moment I appeared had been the advice of her favorite sorcerer: to know that life is hard; that such things happen; that despite the current circumstance the future of her son was bright; that if she—and I as well—stayed focused on our goals, things would all work out.

There are wise men, as I learned from this, in every corner of the world.

And wise women, too.

"What is important in life is moving forward," my mother said to me. "As long as you are in good health, my husband, you will never want for anything."

Again, she nearly came to tears.

It's hard to exaggerate the sustenance that one's relations can provide in the face of calamitous events. From Fungom I returned to Angelina's house full of hope, and resolved to reimagine the path that I would take to reach the goal I'd set. And yet as essential as the words of my relations were, I cannot help feeling that the month of desolation I had suffered at my sister's house had been necessary too. Recovery, after all, cannot begin until the bottom has been reached.

And so I found when I returned to Bamenda that my perspective on the world had changed. The hill I had to climb had not grown lower in my absence, and yet its slopes did not look quite so challenging. As my strength returned I understood that I could not continue very long to live with Christopher and Angelina. I did not have much in common with them, for neither one had had much schooling. Even worse, I could not abide the unrelenting atmosphere of strife. And yet understanding is not the same as being able. To move I needed an apartment; to pay for an apartment I required a job; in Cameroon employment of any substance demands a patron to secure, which, with Pa's abandonment, I'd lost. I can't imagine how life would have been bearable for me there, or how long I might have stayed, or where I would have gone, if not for my sister's acquaintance with the family who lived next door, the head of which, like Christopher, was a policeman.

She knew them from home, I think, for they had come to Bamenda from Sho, the village that abuts Fungom across the Ashing River to the south. Their name was Nenghabi. It was their son—also named Christopher—who made the months there bearable. He was from my world—a boy who had grown up in a mud house but whose parents had been able somehow to send him to school. He was in his second year of high school. Like me he wanted something more from life than the drudgery of mere subsistence, and aspired to go to university.

Christopher was a quiet man, hardworking, a good student. We went on occasion to the movies together, sometimes to church. More often than not we merely talked—about our lives, our ambitions, our dreams. He introduced me to his friends. It was Christopher and they who told me about a program of self-study for a degree with England's Royal Society of Arts that would allow me to earn the diploma I required. With this RSA certificate I could hope for admission to the University of Yaoundé—the nation's most prestigious institution of higher learning.

The commercial college through which I'd study for my RSA certificate provided me with a syllabus and study guide for each course I was to take; all the books I'd need were in the college library. The cost was nominal. And so in this way I looked forward to doing on my own what I had once expected Pa Andrew to help me with.

Among my acquaintances in Bamenda at that time was Emmanuel, the son of Bobe David and Nawain Martha with whom I'd shared a house for many years. He had taken a well-paying job, secured for him by Pa, as a surveyor at a government office in Bamenda, and lived in a nice apartment where I visited him occasionally. Since then he's changed professions to become a well-respected minister. It was from Emmanuel that I first heard how my disgrace had been received in Belo and in Fungom. It was Emmanuel too who professed that his father still believed in me, and that Bobe David had pled my case to Pa on more than one occasion.

Thus it was one day while visiting that I heard from Emmanuel that Pa Andrew had obtained a job for me. Things were like this with Pa. Like a puppet-master hidden from the audience, he pulled the strings of everyone around him without regard for their opinions. After all, I'd waited months without a word to hear that my schooling would continue, and then, suddenly, was informed that I would be going on such-and-such a date to a school—St. Paul's—that I had never heard of. In the same way I now learned that a decision had been made regarding my future in which I'd had no say whatever—and this time not even from Pa himself, but through his sister's son.

I'm sure I expressed to Emmanuel my astonishment at the news, for I could not help being puzzled. Pa Andrew had given the impression that I'd been banished from his family, and never once since he dropped me off at Angelina's had he made an effort to communicate with me. I could only speculate that the counsel of David Cheng had helped to temper Pa's anger. In any case, Emmanuel explained that I was to go to the office of the governor, where all the details would be revealed to me.

How odd this was, I thought. How strange a man was Pa Andrew, how capricious, to wreck a young man's life on the shoals of his mistake, and then, halfheartedly at least, to throw a life ring out to him. I was glad for the opportunity. I badly needed a job. At the governor's office I filled out my application and, in due course, was offered employment at a district office in the town of Fundong. I was not so pleased to hear this, for I had rather stay in Bamenda where I had friends and where I had thought to continue with my studies, than go to a place where I knew no one and had never even been before.

Fundong is a small, provincial town—5,000 or 6,000 people lived there at the time, I'd guess. It lies 100 miles north of Bamenda, past Belo, Mbingo, and Njinikom, and is thought of as a sort of

gateway to the Kom capital of Laikom. But if I'd been displeased
to learn of my assignment, in truth I'm not sure if I could have
found myself in any better circumstance. It happened as Angelina
pointed out to me that our sister Mariam lived not four miles from
Fundong in the village of Fujua, and that an aunt of ours lived
nearby. I was elated. Mariam was among the kindest of my siblings—a stout woman by then, generous and accommodating—
everything, in truth, that Angelina wasn't. In this way I moved
again, to a village little different from Fungom and into a house
with mud walls and a thatched-grass roof exactly like the one
where I'd grown up and where my mother still lived.

The district office was located on the Bamenda Road amid the
rolling farmland of that region, where fields and pastures were
interrupted here and there by copses of woods filled with eucalyptus trees. The office was a sort of county courthouse, whose function was to keep records of land transactions, marriages, births,
and deaths, and to resolve disputes among the local citizenry. As
there were no telephones in Fundong then, the district office was
a busy place, with streams of people going in and coming out from
our opening at 8:00 to closing down at 3:00.

My job was largely clerical—typing, filing, addressing correspondence and mailing it. I did not mind performing as well the
chores of sweeping, mopping, and chopping firewood that my colleagues thought beneath them. There were five of them besides
our director. They were a lazy lot, all older than I, who smoked
heavily and went out drinking every afternoon to the off-license
joints that stood about the market square. There they tipped bottles of Gold Harp or Beaufort to their lips, called out to their
friends, bought hard boiled eggs or shish kabobs off of women
passing through the market with their trays. For all I know they
might have patronized as well the prostitutes who worked the
market too, unhindered by the law. My colleagues were not an ill-

natured lot. They were always pestering me to go out with them and if they saw me they'd wave me over to their tables. I joined them occasionally for the sake of good relations and remember buying rounds now and then. For the most part though I avoided the genial beer drinkers in the market square, preferring round-about paths to home.

If my colleagues thought me standoffish for refusing to join them in their celebrations, still I was never ostracized at work. The atmosphere was congenial. My boss was fair. At noon other ladies bearing trays appeared with meals of beans and plantains, rice and yams which could be had for 100 francs CFA a plate, and which were really very good. From my arrival at 8:00 I filed papers and opened envelopes without complaint, expecting little more than a paycheck in return. When 3:00 arrived I could close my drawers, stand up, and leave the office without further obligation until morning.

Only one experience at the Fundong district office stands out as memorable. It was discovered one day some months into my tenure that 400,000 Cameroonian francs—$1,000 more or less—were missing from a locked drawer whose keys were held by the director and his two private secretaries. One of these secretaries, the only woman in the office, was not the sort to steal even an avocado from the market, let alone so great a sum of money, and our suspicions fell naturally on the other.

The police were called in. When no one confessed to this con-siderable crime everybody in our office, as well as seven employ-ees from the town's Municipal Council Office, were hauled off to jail. No sort of investigation was undertaken. It was expected I think that if the criminal were confined some time with his col-leagues he could not help but to confess the deed.

We were held five days, eating and drinking only what our relatives might carry in to us. As with the bananas, the mangoes, and the oranges at the Belo Primary School, we all shared equally. Our relations served us steaming dishes of fufu corn and njama-njama, and cups of water poured from calabashes that they had carried to our cell.

At night we slept shirtless on the jail's concrete floor. During the day we were released into the station's yard to mill about, enduring such boredom as I could never have recalled were it not for a photograph taken at the time—by whom I don't remember—of me and a colleague, Joseph Mbah, sitting on the station steps. We're wearing identical bell-bottomed trousers but neither shirts nor shoes, both very dark-skinned men, both well-muscled. In this image Joe is staring at the ground with a resignation that one sees in every third-world country from those who've been caught up in the arms of an uneven legal system—an expression which, were it not for the evidence before me, I would have supposed to be my own. In fact, though, I'm slouched against the station wall, my legs extended, my ankles crossed, my arms folded before me in a sort of casual rebuke to the injustice of the law. Far from resigned, my expression is defiant, even amused a little at this charade being acted by the authorities, staring into the lens and thus into the future with a self-assurance that one can only have as, on the cusp of adulthood, he believes utterly in himself. It's the expression in that photograph which more than anything reminds me of the single-minded determination that possessed me then to make something of my life.

As for the crime of stealing $1,000, we were soon released for lack of evidence. My colleagues later hired the services of a sorcerer to identify the culprit. But though the sorcerer is said to have fingered the man we all knew to be guilty, no one was ever charged.

In Fundong I became the secretary of the church which I had joined, and, like my mother with her friends in their little credit union, the secretary of the local Njangi. I was treated by my sister's neighbors in little Fujua as a scholar, a celebrity, an important man. The villagers there, most of them illiterate, came to me to read to them the governmental notices that they'd received, to explain these missives, and to compose whatever responses were required. Beyond my powers as a government authority, I possessed a flashlight that was considered nearly magical, and a shortwave radio that was idolized.

Mariam had four children, the oldest of whom, Martin, who was 11 at the time and in primary school, had a severe learning disability. I tutored him in English and arithmetic, and swatted him when he skipped school or failed to do his homework. Mariam was grateful, I think, for my appearance in her life just then. She had besides the worries over Martin two debilitating ailments— stomach pains, which went undiagnosed, and toothaches that were never treated. I recall very clearly how I cringed each night as my sister cried in pain, how sad I felt that there was nothing I could do about it.

I was never lonely in Fundong. I never felt an outsider as I had with Pa Andrew and his sister. Mariam and her children adored me. My Auntie Amina Chousinjah and her husband, Bobe Titang, lived not far away in a huge compound with Bobe Titang's five other wives and their many children. Auntie sometimes fed me special meals—of crayfish, say, and a vegetable called "bitter leaf," seasoned with something called a "Magicube" that was wrapped in a foil package like bouillon.

In Fundong I made friends as well—one in particular, Augustine Tedji, who worked for the police department issuing national identity cards and was putting his little brother through secondary school. They shared an apartment in Fundong Three Corners where I sometimes stayed if we'd gone out to the nightclubs or the bars with other friends of ours and I had no desire to make the 45 minute walk to Fugua.

I even had a girlfriend for a while—an elementary schoolteacher whom I thought quite beautiful. I had met her in Bamenda, where she was a part of the Kom community to which Angelina and her husband belonged. We were occasional lovers and went dancing sometimes at the People's Bar, one of two nightclubs in the Fundong market square. I loved her in a way, and I know that she was fond of me.

However pleasant my time in Fundong, though, I was not there to file papers or to chop wood or to tutor children or to look at pretty girls. I was there to study for my RSA exams and to leave the place behind in favor of academic study in Yaoundé and the pursuit of my dream of going to America. Without the work, the friends, the relatives, I no doubt would have been miserable. With them to support me, though, I can say honestly that the most pleasant memories I have of that time are of the reading I did most evenings in economics, history, commerce, and geography. I had early on found a spot outdoors where I could study, and which in time I became connected to in an almost spiritual way. It was a granite outcropping on the side of steep hill, flat, backed by a stand of eucalyptus trees, and with stunning views across the little Fugua River of the valley floor below, its farms, its pastures and its woods, the mountains rising on the other side, the clouds overhead and their shadows running on the ground below.

The hard work on my granite rock nourished my curiosity to understand the wider world as well as to see it for myself one day, beyond the water too big to swim across whose fish would eat you up. I was elated when I learned after taking my exams that I had passed—elated, but unsurprised, because the time to learn which those quiet evenings gave me had come rather as a gift than a burden to be borne.

CHAPTER TWELVE

The University of Yaoundé was, for an English speaker like myself who did not have a fluency in French, as chaotic and intimidating as it was a thrilling place to be. Fifteen thousand students—some of them from wealthy families such as I had never known—walked about in large tight groups, confident, casual, and worldly-wise. There was then as well from the inauguration of a new president, Paul Biya, an air of excitement that one could not help being caught up in. For we Anglophones this was especially true, since Biya—himself a native French speaker—was the first president of Cameroon to address the nation in the English language.

The students at the university were a rowdy bunch. Courses of 500 and more were taught in either of two amphitheaters on the campus, where a kind of bedlam reigned. The place was a mess, with trash strewn everywhere and the toilets often clogged. Serious students like myself—in my memory at least, more of them native English than French speakers—sat down front to better hear the lectures. In the upper levels students came and went as if passing through a subway stop at rush hour. They called to their friends. They heckled the teachers. They threw pens and wads of paper. The more obnoxious of the men shouted horrible insults at the women in the crowd, laughing and calling them things like *"laboratoires de SIDA"*—AIDS laboratories.

The classes that were taught in French I had difficulty with unless they focused, like mathematics and economics, on numbers. Classes taught in English and their professors were my favorites. I remember especially my family law teacher, Dr. Ngwafor, and Dr. Aletom who taught sociology, and Dr. Ayangwe with his big afro whom the French students mocked for being what they called "too proud."

When not at school I lived in one of the more affluent of Yaoundé's neighborhoods—a community called Madagascar that looks down on the city from the slopes of one among its seven hills. Another of Pa Andrew's far-flung protégés, a man called Innocent—unrelated to the journalist of the same name—lived with his wife, their two young girls, and two of his brothers and his sister, in an apartment that stood above a patisserie. I had met Innocent at Pa's house once or twice, and when I happened to run into him in Fundong one day—he had come on business, I believe—I asked whether I might live with him.

"Sure!" he said. "Come along!"

He really was quite personable.

At Innocent's house I shared a bed with one of his brothers. The apartment was comfortable; it stood close by a metro stop; it possessed a veranda with a splendid view. In the dry season dust rose in clouds from the heavily traveled street below, where the American ambassador in his beautiful black Lincoln Continental could be seen whizzing by. Whatever else one might say about the French, their food, adapted to the tastes and produce of Cameroon, was superb. There was an off-license establishment across the street that served a dish of grilled plantains and plums whose memory still makes me salivate, and cups of toasted corn.

Innocent was a grandson of the late Fon of Kom. His father, who bore the title "Prince," was a wealthy, influential man, the head of the Kom political party and an owner of motels in Belo and Fundong. Innocent himself worked in the Community Development Office where Pa had hired him, I imagine, as a favor to his father. In addition to the development work Innocent ran from his apartment a side business in which his brothers and I helped, securing government loans for honest people to buy their cars and houses.

I thought when I arrived that Innocent Chia must be very good at his job, for his customers were numerous. They streamed in and out at all hours of the day and night looking for him, though he never seemed to be there when they called. Soon enough they began to berate me for his absence. In time I learned that these customers were less interested in paying bills than they were in being paid the money out of which, they uniformly claimed, he'd cheated them. And yet despite the abuse I suffered as my landlord's surrogate, I felt warmly welcomed in his house. Nor could I help being impressed by the industry and cleverness he showed in avoiding his clientele. Even later, when I myself fell victim to one of his scams, I could not hold too large a grudge against the man.

Innocent Chia was the most likable crook I've ever known.

Besides my attendance at the university, and the job of fending off disgruntled customers, my chief occupation during this period of my life was dreaming of America and scheming how to get there. Yaoundé offered greater opportunities for immersing myself in the culture of America than anywhere I'd lived. At the Etoug Ebe Baptist Church in the neighborhood of Messa, I made a point of sitting near an American nurse who worked at a nearby hospital. At the *Palais de Congrès* I attended concerts with

American performers. Sometimes on a whim I'd take the bus to the Yaoundé airport, just to watch planes take off and think: someday that will be me on that plane, flying to America.

At other times I took the bus downtown just to gaze at the American Embassy with its stars and stripes fluttering above and to watch the people going in and out. I was jealous of them. I thought, "Maybe one day that will be me." Back and forth I'd stroll before the building imagining America with such focus that at times I felt I was standing on its soil; that I had come somehow to be already living the American dream; that I had been transformed by magic into a lucky citizen.

In time I found my way to the American Cultural Center, an arm of the U.S. government whose mission was to promote the country to people like myself, in a nice stone building downtown that soon became for me a sort of home away from home. The staff were helpful, friendly, generous. The Center possessed a small library and a quiet, air-conditioned environment where I brought my books to study.

One of the most helpful of my friends at the Center was a woman whose name I never learned, and whom I took at first to be African American, since, though white, she had extremely curly, close-cropped hair. It was she who suggested that I apply to American colleges—an idea that had not occurred to me. Studying abroad was considered more prestigious by far than attendance at any institution in Cameroon. Even those who graduate from the University of Yaoundé aspire to go elsewhere for degrees—to Nigeria, to Europe and America.

"What sort of school would suit you best?" she asked.

A small university, I told her—I did not then understand the difference between universities and colleges—where I could get more individual attention.

She gave me a single application, to Westbrook College near Portland, Maine, which, in retrospect, was as unlikely a place for a Cameroonian immigrant to attain a higher education as it was possible to imagine. I have no idea why she picked that school out of the scores of liberal arts colleges in the United States. The Westbrook College administrators were puzzled too. Had she grown up in Maine? Was she herself a graduate of the place? But neither I nor they would ever know how the decision would be made that would shape the course of my existence.

The woman told me what I'd need to apply to the college's School of Business Administration. She helped me through the mountains of paperwork and even paid the application fee herself in return for my promise to reimburse her. There weren't any essays to write. I mailed to Westbrook College the diplomas, the RSA scores, the results of my TOEFL exam, a check—and then began to wait.

The hours, the days, the weeks that passed before I heard of the college's decision were among the most endless of my life. I wallowed in the same mud of self-pity into which I'd fallen on returning by train from Douala to Yaoundé, in shame from Pa's recalling me. I began to doubt myself. How could I, an orphan raised in a mud hut, hope to be flying to America in two months' time to study at a college there? It seemed the remotest of possibilities—a joke, even, that the woman at the Cultural Center was playing on a poor black man like me. As everyone does from time to time I felt utterly alone. I was no more than a servant, I decided—a servant who'd been taken like a stray cat into the homes of successful people, to be fed and housed but never loved. It seemed to me that if I was not accepted at an American college I'd have no place to go except to Belo; that the struggle and the hardships would have been endured for nothing; and that I might be left to a life of cutting weeds and picking corn and tilling the earth from whence I'd come.

"*Matimiwu?*" I asked myself as my mother had so often. "What is to become of me?"

It was in this mood of despair that I answered the door at my home one day to find that Pa Andrew had come to call. His presence astonished me. I hadn't seen him in years—in fact, since he and Mama dropped me on the dusty road before my sister's house. He seemed to have forgotten his mistreatment of me and was solicitous of my well-being. He congratulated me on the successful completion of my high school exams. He inquired how my studies at the university were going and about what progress had been made on the acceptance of my RSA certificate. I thanked him for the job he'd gotten me in Fundong and for all the rest that he had done for me. I didn't trust him, though. I couldn't bring myself to tell him of my Westbrook College application, from the fear of his laughing at my prospects, I suppose, and from the suspicion too that he might use his connections in the government to thwart my ambitions.

Not long after that a letter came informing me that I had been accepted to the college. I couldn't credit it at first. I read and re-read the letter to make certain I had not misunderstood, and scanned the form enclosed with it allowing me to obtain a student visa. Such forms, the so-called I-20, are so coveted that in most third-world countries a black market has long existed in the things. I knew people who had waited years for one, unsuccessfully. I was so elated that I went around to all my friends waiving it about. That was the token—a piece of printed paper, cheap, fragile, given without feeling or concern for who I was—that represented then, as it does even now, the achievement of a lifelong goal.

Ambition is a curious thing, whose power burns intensely inside us, like a fire beneath a boiler, to motivate us and to help us persevere. Without ambition I would have been content to farm for the rest of my life a piece of Uncle Diffrey's land. Without it I would not have found Jane Austen or the feeling of home that an immigrant from Africa can have in Portland, Maine. And yet as far as it can take us no matter how high we might reach, ambition always has an end. And we have reached at last the summit of our aspirations, we must ask ourselves, "What then?" When we have become the doctor, the lawyer, the astronaut—the President of the United States—we cannot help wondering what will we do next.

My story is about ambition and achievement, but it's also a story about what is left to fill us up when they have been fulfilled.

CHAPTER THIRTEEN

The train that runs between Yaoundé and Douala passes through the heart of Cameroon. This is not true in the geographical sense, for Yaoundé lies less than a third of the way from the sea to the country's eastern border. In social, cultural, and economic senses, though, the land between the country's two largest cities is what most Cameroonians think of when they think of Cameroon. A train running through this country passes through farms and equatorial rainforests and through a mountain pass of 1,300 feet, before winding its way down to the sea. It crosses the country's largest river—the Sanaga—which flows some 500 miles from its headwaters in the eastern mountains, and along which the vast majority of Cameroon's population lives.

In this way, in September, 1987, soon after I'd turned 21, I took my leave of the world I knew on a path to the world of which all my life I'd dreamt, whose images on film and television were the bases of a meager understanding of my destination. The day was unbearably hot, the air thick and sultry. Whatever breezes might be sighing in my old neighborhood of Madagascar had not found their ways to Yaoundé's downtown train station. Crowds of people moved in inscrutable crosscurrents to catch or leave their trains: a chaos of humanity—businessmen in shiny shoes and ur-chins in rags; sellers of fruit, water, tea, and trinkets—and a ca-cophony of French, pidgin English, and a host of native tongues.

The train was dirty, down at heel.

The people, though, were friendly.

"*Bonjour, comment ça va?*" the passengers in my compartment asked.

"*Bien,*" was my reply. I was shy of my French.

"*Comment tu t'appelles?*" they inquired politely.

"*Je m'appelle* Richard," I answered back.

Then they would speak to me in English.

Any trip by train in Cameroon is not for the faint of heart. The noise of the beasts alone defies adequate description. Their whis-tles, their struggling engines, the screeching of their breaks and the rumble of their wheels on uneven tracks—all of these are louder and more grating on the nerves than on the trains that I've encountered since. Accidents on the Cameroon National Railway system are common. Trains derail at astonishing rates, killing doz-ens, scores, once even hundreds of people at a time. Trains carry-ing diesel fuel and gasoline, running off the tracks, explode in such spectacular fashion that videos of the blazes are carried on news-casts around the world.

One can understand, then, something of the fervor with which, as we set off, I prayed to God and Jesus Christ that such a fate would not befall me. On my first train trip in Cameroon, following Pa's recalling me from the Reverend Yongkuma's house to his, I had been too traumatized to think of what other disasters might await me. Now though, fully in my senses, I imagined the train flying off its tracks at each rolling turn. Every screech foretold the explosion that must follow. When we passed through the first tunnel I recalled an incident in which soccer fans returning to Douala, and, unable to find seats, clung to the train's sides like bees on a hive, were knocked off and killed at that very spot.

My fellow passengers, thankfully, seemed unconcerned with Camrail's checkered history. They were more frequent travelers than I, and so had banished any thoughts of catastrophe in favor of light banter and the reading of their newspapers, magazines, and books. From time to time they spoke to me in broken English and offered up such food as they had brought along. And as we left Yaoundé, past the lines of palm trees and timber shacks with rusty cars out front, I too settled down into the mood of contemplation that always accompanies such trips, into an unknown future, terribly exciting if at times a little frightening.

As I sat my mind wandered, tracing back over the events of the last few days.

I recalled the thrill of buying my airplane tickets—first to Paris, thence to Washington, D.C., from there eventually to Portland. The travel agent was a friendly man, slightly bald and so heavy that he could raise himself from his chair only with difficulty. With a patience that even then I thought remarkable, he explained everything to me: how to transfer between the two Paris airports; the reservation I had at a Holiday Inn in Washington, where I would have to overnight. I couldn't fathom any of it. I had never once in my 21 years crossed the borders of my country, or flown on any sort of plane.

"Portland, Maine!" I thought to myself as with my newly purchased airplane tickets I made my way home, to the house I shared with Innocent Chia and his family. I said the city's name over and over again, as if the repetition would make the place my home. "Portland! Portland! Portland, Maine!"

On the train now I held in my lap a map of the United States, where I'd be able to track my progress to Maine from the nation's capital. In Fungom, in Belo, I had never seen a map, let alone needed one. I merely walked, up and down the hills and mountainsides whose forked paths I knew as one knows the way to the front door of his house. It seemed impossible to me that I would one day know my new home as well as I knew the smells, the sounds, the running rivers, and the peculiar sunlight of my native one.

How sad it was to leave all that behind.

In Fungom when I arrived to tell my relatives and friends goodbye, I found that the news of my good luck had traveled before me on the puzzling currents of communication that are so much a part of oral cultures. Even for those of us who have grown up in remote villages, the means by which news travels can at times seem unfathomable. From Yaoundé to Bamenda, from Bamenda to Belo, from Belo up the path through Kikfuini and Sho, word of my departure had come to Fungom without my sending it.

It had occurred to me more than once that the trip to America and the future that awaited me held so many unknowns that I could not be sure I'd ever see my family again. And yet I hadn't imagined the sadness I would feel at seeing them, or the joy they would have for me at my success, or the warmth of their affection. Uncle Diffrey, stooping in his garden, was the first to see me walking up the path.

"Richard! How much you've grown!" he exclaimed, exactly as if I were ten years old and had been gone a year or more.

How happy he had been to hear of my good fortune! How certainly he had known all along that I was destined for great things!

He took my arm at once and began to lead me up the hill to Mother's house. A neighbor appeared, who showed the same elation at my arrival that Uncle Diffrey had. Soon others, hearing the commotion, began to follow us, babbling and calling out the news of my arrival, exclaiming over my new shirt and trousers, my extravagant new shoes. I might have been Michael Jackson walking up that hill in Fungom that day, for all the clamor I aroused. I think too that a measure of their excitement was anticipation of the expression on my mother's face when she saw who had arrived.

I stopped a little way before I reached our house. I don't know why. It's possible that I too, like our friends, wished to witness the expected exclamations that could not help ensuing when my mother saw me standing there. My mother has always been a bit of a drama queen.

In any case, we were not disappointed.

"My Lord!" she yelped when she appeared on her veranda to see what was going on outside. "You are home! My Ayeah is home! Praise the Lord!"

She nearly knocked me over hugging me.

The two days I spent in Fungom were among the sweetest of my life. The friends, the neighbors who stopped by to wish me well took pride in my accomplishments, for as they justly felt they had had a part in raising me.

At Uncle Seing's we shared the kola nut and cup of palm wine that are so much a part of leave-takings with the Kom. My uncle reminded me of my responsibilities. He who, besides my mother and my Uncle Diffrey, had had the greatest part in raising me, wished to take some credit for my success—a credit which I gladly gave. The scene was quite emotional. My uncle nearly cried. What struck me too about this goodbye was his reminder that my setting off for college in America was the greatest moment not just of my life, but of my mother's too. For this she had given up so much. For this she had struggled as a single mother in a world where the lot of single mothers was among the most difficult on earth.

I told Uncle Seing how grateful I was for his having built my mother's house and given her some land to farm. I knew, I said, that without his help our family would surely have been scattered to the winds, and could hardly imagine how difficult our lives would have been without his kindness and his generosity.

He died in Fungom a year ago, as I write these words just now, at the age of something over 100.

I cried when I heard the news.

Mother was so sweet to me while I remained in Fungom that I myself nearly came to tears. She cooked me special meals of coco-yams and okra soup, and fussed about me as if I were not merely her son, her husband, the father of her children, the prince she'd raised from infancy, but a king whose domain reached across the broad blue seas which she had heard about but could not imagine.

Most of all, though, she counseled the humility that was the center of her philosophy of life, and repeated the advice that she had given me so many times before: that I must never forget my roots; that I was the head of our family; that I bore responsibility not just for her, but for my siblings. She admonished me to take care of myself, and in this way to thwart the efforts of those evil spirits who are the causes of life's most trying times.

I had in mind that we would say our goodbyes in Fungom, and that I would make my way alone to Belo to stop with Bobe David to thank him too for all that he had done for me.

My mother, though, had other plans. She wanted to come with me, she said. And so when she had gathered her belongings we set off together, down the path that I'd first traveled at the age of four when she carried me to school. Just then I could see the valley of the Mughom River from those same childish eyes, the sort of view that never fails to fill me with awe. I grieved at the thought of leaving it behind, for even if I should return, this world, the peaceful village, the view that I had now, the easy feeling of walking there beside my mother would never be the same. I impressed on my mind not just the picture of this beautiful world but the feeling of it too, so that years hence I would not regret forgetting it. Such moments are rare in our lives when we know that we will never see our homes again as we are seeing them just now. It's important to do this, to take the time, in a world where the future and the past claim so many minutes of our lives, to take the time to remember its most ecstatic moments.

In Belo when I arrived with Mother I thanked Bobe David for all that he had done. I saw myself everywhere: in the boys who stood across the way from the Maternity Center to watch the people come and go, who helped their elders selling clothing in the market, who made their ways to the Belo school in uniforms of khaki shorts and green shirts well tucked in. In the firm sure grip of Bobe David's hand I felt a child again. In his house I could almost see my ghost lying on the kitchen floor and hear once more the voice of Martha scolding me. She was on her best behavior now, as I could tell because she smiled at me and offered up her cheek to kiss.

Again, with David, I heard from a relation how proud he was of me. Again, as with my Uncle Seing, we nearly came to tears. David read from the Bible and led us all in prayer. And though I could never repay him for his kindnesses and for the character that he had helped to build in me, I did express my thanks. I felt as well a kind of grudging regard even for his wife, for Nawain Martha in her way had had a good deal to do with making the man I had become, in testing my resolve.

My mother cried when it was time for her to make the long walk home up the mountainside.

"*Ndzi*," "*Nyah*," "*Matimewu*," she called me, just as she had when I was a child. "Husband," "Father," "Son."

She told me that she loved me more than she loved her own life; that she was prouder of me than I could ever know; that I had brought her more joy than she could ever have imagined.

"You have traveled Cameroon and touched many lives, helped many people of ours," she told me as she took my hands. "You have always done this with a smile, and rarely complained or made me mad at you. You are my hope, my precious seed planted in this world—the seed of my life, the seed that made your family. Wherever you go, Ayeah, be strong. Hold fast to the values you have learned and remember that I will always love you."

My mother spit into my upturned palms, first one, then the other, and pressed my hands together, and told me as she had so many times before that in this part of her I would find whenever obstacles appeared the strength that she had given me.

I held these memories tightly to me on the train from Yaoundé to Douala, as I watched the landscape rattle by. Here at a railroad crossing a man on a motor scooter waited patiently for us to pass. There girls in print dresses waved to us. We passed trainloads of eucalyptus, mahogany, and teak logs waiting on their sidings; villages identical to Fungom; miles and miles of jungle thickets. At tiny railroad stations when we stopped men and women approached the train with trays of plantains held above their heads, basketsful of mangoes, oranges, tangerines, and lemons, bottles of water—all for sale to eager hands reaching from the windows of our car.

This was Cameroon: roads of red dirt; dilapidated houses and scruffy farms; sweeping, gorgeous views; the beauty, the energy, the happy smiles of home. I watched the people we passed by—a man walking with the steady purpose of one who has many miles to go; a woman with a basket on her head; a group of boys swinging cutlasses in savage strokes to keep the weeds at bay—and could see myself in all of them. And though I could not foretell the future, though I couldn't know what else I might become, I knew that until I took my last breath on earth this was what I was.

In the clattering train I could not help smiling as I remembered my last trip to visit Pa Andrew. I had thought it only right that I stop to thank him for his part in helping me along my way to a future, which, despite his anger at my supposed ingratitude, I could never otherwise have found. The family had moved once more, to a house in Bamenda much like the two that I had shared with them.

When I arrived I found to my surprise that not only was I greeted warmly, but that Pa had set a scene of sorts—his whole family in attendance around the living room—in which to make sure they heard his praise of me. Even now so many years removed from that set piece, I am more than a little puzzled by the shift in his view of me, as if a large ship, having once reversed its westward course, now faced the setting sun again.

He told the family I was exceptional.

They all sat quietly listening.

He told them that no one in his house had ever achieved what I had now achieved, and that, of all the boys whom he'd supported through the years—feeding and clothing them, sending them to school—not one had gone on to a college in America.

I don't know whether his family had heard all this before, or whether, like me, it came as a surprise that one who had once faced disgrace was now a model of perseverance in the face of much adversity.

If that had been the end of Pa's pronouncements I would have left the place with a warm regard for him and all his family. But Pa wasn't finished. He told them that it would make them all feel good inside to take credit for the success that I'd achieved, but that, in fact, I had done it on my own, and he himself had been among the obstacles that I had had to overcome.

I was astonished. It wasn't just that I had never seen these qualities in Pa—humility, regret, apology—but that they should be directed at one like me who had once been nothing more than the orphan in their house, the bastard, the obligation to be borne. With these words I, who had felt so much an outsider in their presence, had been admitted to the family.

On the train now, reflecting on that day, I wondered how one could not help feeling touched by such honest apology, and considered that just as Pa had admitted me to his family, I had admitted him to mine. From him, from my mother, from Bobe David and my uncles, I had so much to be grateful for that I wondered whether it would be possible to fully thank them. Many immigrants tell a story of how weighty are the expectations that their relatives have for them, how heavy are the burdens of their obligations. But as the train rolled toward Douala I remember feeling that from my own relatives I'd had nothing but the warmest wishes for my success, without obligation, without the expectation of a return on their investment.

The thought of leaving Cameroon was bittersweet. Whatever awaited me across the ocean, I would miss much of what it was that I was hoping to escape. I would miss the sounds of crickets chirping by the millions. I would miss the mountains of my native land and the sweeping views that they afford. I would miss the pleasure one takes in a plate of fufu corn and njamma-njamma, which can only be appreciated after a hard days' labor, in a mud and thatched-grass hut, beside a fire of eucalyptus embers. I watched the land pass by—my land, forever—with no less sadness than I'd had in parting with my mother and my uncles. I watched the families walking barefoot back and forth beside the tracks, the laundry that fluttered from sagging lines, the placid, muddy streams we crossed—I watched, and wondered whether I would ever see these things again.

CHAPTER FOURTEEN

At the Douala airport I was greeted by a disorder that made even the chaos of the train station seem tame. The airport at that time was a dilapidated, low-slung affair, whose walls, though they had been erected scarcely ten years earlier, were cracked, and whose paint was already peeling. Peddlers abounded in every corner, yammering in French and pressing their trinkets and their clothing, their plaster-of-Paris figures, their billfolds made from the skins of exotic animals, on everyone who passed. At each step another hand reached out to help me with my luggage.

The day was hot. The air was filled with the salty odors of the ocean, thick, humid, and oppressive. My suitcases were heavy, so that from time to time against my better judgment I was forced to set them down. The Douala airport for any honest person was at that time a dangerous locale—a place filled not only with the pushy vendors, but with pickpockets, con-artists, thieves and other rascals. I worried that my suitcase might be grabbed and whisked away. I feared for the safety of my wallet. With my handkerchief I wiped my brow, lifted up my luggage, and once more shouldered my way through the crowd.

The fear for my luggage, my money, my person, though, was nothing compared with my growing apprehension of the flight itself. Ever since a child watching the airplanes flying overhead, I had wanted to be in one. To sail away in that deep blue sky of Cameroon's dry season, above the swiftly passing land, seemed to me so fantastical that I could not imagine anything more thrilling.

And yet from the moment I had bought my ticket in Yaoundé, the idea nagged at me that as easily as a plane might rise, so it might fall. Even as I took my boarding pass, even as I watched my luggage set onto a conveyor belt—itself miraculous, for I'd never heard of such a thing before—my stomach throbbed as I considered my impending doom: the feeling of terror as my plane fell from the sky; the regret at a life cut short before my dreams were realized; the crash, my body crushed; the ensuing explosion and a fiery end to life.

At the airplane's door I found the captain greeting everyone who boarded—robust, confident, for a moment smiling warmly at me alone, as if we'd known each other for years. Beside him two flight attendants directed the shuffling passengers to their seats. These attendants were young and beautiful, and dressed in the tailored uniforms that only Air France could require of its employees. The French they spoke was lovely, flawless. Their smiles, like the captain's, were so genuine and so reassuring that for a moment my fear was dissipated.

At last, through the pressing mass of people, I found my seat. Across the aisle sat a girl not much more than ten, whose toes barely reached the floor, and yet whose self-possession and easy manner struck me as improbable. How could one so young, I wondered, await our departure with such aplomb? When I was told to buckle my seatbelt, I did so with the energy of one who thinks of seatbelts as the only things that stand between them and certain death. The engines started. Their noise was terrible. In proportion to their rising rumble my terror grew, so that even now, years later, I know that I have never felt so frightened in my life. The lights went off. In the gloom I felt exactly as I had once imagined I would feel in the dark belly of that bird, trapped, doomed, the sweat rising on my forehead, my breathing rapid as if for lack of oxygen, my bag clutched tightly in my lap.

Soon enough the plane was roaring down the runway at a speed that I had never felt before and had not considered as something that might be added to my terror. My back was pressed into the seat. My breathing grew more shallow. It was true that a number of my fellow passengers were no less terrified than I, and I took some comfort from their looks of horror, and from the signs of the cross that they were making in the air before them.

We frightened few, though, were exceptions to the rule of calm. For most the experience of roaring down a runway at such high speed appeared to be no less ordinary than that of strolling down the street. Most of my fellows had closed their eyes, or they had opened up a book, or they were chatting comfortably with those in the seats beside them, as if death were not awaiting us.

The little girl across the aisle wore an almost beatific smile. Her parents, if they had joined her on this trip, were nowhere to be seen.

"Is this your first time on an airplane, sir?" she inquired of me politely.

I admitted that it was.

"I thought so. Isn't it fun!?"

There was something so innocent about this child—her dangling legs, her honest confidence—that I found my own confidence returning. The airplane lifted off the ground, and yet I lived. The buildings and the cars which so recently had been familiar, grew smaller, and yet there were my bag still safely in my hands, my feet planted on the floor, the girl smiling across the aisle. My breathing grew more regular. The sweat on my forehead dried. From the girl to my surprise I saw that I had found a courage that I hadn't known existed. Soon enough I knew that she was right.

"Yes!" I told her. "Yes—it's very fun!"

From that moment I too was a seasoned traveler.

The flight to France was uneventful.

In Paris I changed airports, in order to change planes.

And though the sights of France were new to me—the Eiffel Tower, beautiful as I saw it from the sky; the hallways of Le Bourget and Charles de Gaulle immaculate, the clerks there helpful and friendly—in my mind they could not be a tenth as wondrous as the monuments, the buildings, the hallways and the clerks in the United States would be.

I was still infatuated with the idea of America as the land of plenty, with which no other country on the earth could possibly compare.

And when at last I saw Washington, D.C.—the Capitol just there below me!—I nearly cried. There it was, glistening in the morning sunlight as if recently scrubbed down, calm, peaceful, awaiting the newest of its immigrants.

Of my arrival in America, my sweetest memory is of clearing customs. I was extremely nervous, as every honest person is for reasons that aren't clear to me. So far as I knew I had brought no contraband along. My papers were in order. And yet there I was waiting to be turned away like an insect who had no right to enter such a lovely, healthful place as I imagined America to be.

The official who took my passport, it happened, was African-American. And though black like me, he spoke English as his native tongue, with the accents of America that I had thus far heard only from the lips of white people who had come to work in Cameroon. He took my passport and looked deeply into my eyes, for signs, I guess, of furtiveness or guilt. It seemed to me that my fate lay in his hands; that he alone of the earth's billions of inhabitants had the power to determine the course of my existence.

Many immigrants—most, even, as I think about it now—have felt just the way that I did then. And yet I'm quite sure that the man who stood before me as the keeper of the gate was among the people of this world who take time to consider everyone whom they encounter as unique. It was for me one of those moments that remain forever fixed in our minds, with the greatest clarity and sense of awe that life can hold such forces. Perhaps my emotions were so heightened that I saw in this man all the goodness that I expected of Americans, but it seemed to me—and I can still see this clearly—that a tear came to his eye to see that someone's lifelong dream was just then being realized.

And then he said my name and bid me welcome to the country, and stamped my passport, and watched me walk into America.

I found my luggage. A taxi took me to the Holiday Inn where I had a reservation.

I had been in America a halfhour I guess when we arrived at my hotel. Until that moment nothing about the country had differed much from what I'd known before. The airport had been no different from those that I had seen in France. A taxi is a taxi, after all. But now in the lobby of the inn where I would spend the night, my experience with the wonders of America began. I was handed a plastic card and instructions on how to find my room, but given no key to unlock its door. I carried my luggage down a hallway to my door. I tried the handle, but found it wouldn't move. I stood there for a time, my brows knitted in puzzlement at how I should be admitted. The plastic card held no significance to me. I suppose I'd thought that the room would be unlocked—that America was a place of such spectacular honesty that no doors anywhere were locked. I tried the handle once again, and again I was rebuffed.

I nodded to myself. I thought. In time I picked my suitcase up and trudged back to the front desk to explain.

The clerk smiled in an understanding way, for he'd doubtless run across others who had never seen a plastic key before.

He walked me to my room. He showed me how the mechanism worked. I thanked him and went in.

I could not credit my senses as I looked about the place, for I had never been in such a fine room as that. The towels, so white they might have been brand new, hung from spotless racks. The floor was so clean that it reflected the bright lights of the place, and it troubled me to think how I could walk across its tiles without dirtying it. The mirror! I had never seen such a flawless mirror, or had ever had a clearer image of myself. The toilet shone no less than the floor it stood upon, the water in its bowl so clean, so pure, that anyone in Cameroon would have gladly drunk from it.

In the shower I washed off the dirt and weariness of travel beneath a constant stream of water—and even so, when I turned down the covers of my bed and saw the brightness of its sheets, I could hardly bring myself to sleep on them. In time I compromised, vowing to take up the merest sliver of the bed, with care to avoid befouling the greater part of it.

This was the most luxurious room that I had ever seen before, let alone been in. And it was mine for the night's entirety!

In the morning by taxi I made my way once more to the airport. I found the gate from which my plane to Portland was to leave.

"Portland, Maine!" I thought again, as I had thought when I bought my tickets in Yaoundé. "Portland! Portland! Portland, Maine!"

We would not be flying straight to my destination for I would have to change planes one last time. I knew, though, that I was getting close.

And so with the excitement of anyone who has come so close to realizing a dream, I boarded our plane to Denver, Colorado.

I knew where Denver was. I'd read the word many times on the map I purchased in Yaoundé and had carried with me ever since. Indeed there can have hardly been a human being in the world who had traced the path as many times as I, from Washington, D.C. to Denver, from Denver to the country's eastern seaboard once again. Nor had this itinerary failed to strike me as strange—an inefficiency that I had not associated with the country of my dreams. And yet there it was. Like the drinking water in the toilet bowl, I must accept that in America one must fly halfway across a continent and back again to reach his destination.

The trip itself was unremarkable, for I was by now accustomed to long flights.

A half hour or so before we were to land, a lady sitting in the seat behind my own inquired where I was going.

"To Portland!" I replied.

"Which Portland?" she inquired.

"Why, Portland, Maine," I answered.

I held up the map that I had carried with me from Douala, and pointed to my destination. I showed her the brochure I held of Westbrook College.

It was only then that my mistake was revealed: that my itinerary was to take me to Portland, Oregon, instead; that, indeed, there must have been planes flying from Washington to Maine; that no one knowingly would make the trip by way of Colorado.

Everything was sorted out in time. The lady explained my plight to a flight attendant. The flight attendant carried this news to the clerks inside the airport. They arranged to fly me to Portland, Maine, through Chicago, Illinois.

My luggage never found me though. I guess its fate all along had been to venture out to Oregon, and thence into a void where all the world's lost luggage lives.

And thus it was that, three days late and weary from my trip, I found my way to Portland, Maine, to Westbrook College, and to a new life in the land I'd dreamt so often of.

CHAPTER FIFTEEN

To my eyes fresh to the sights of America, Westbrook College was a lovely, tranquil refuge from the poverty, the prejudice, the ignorance and crumbling infrastructure that I had known at home. It thrilled me to have landed in such a place, where the grass was cut, the sidewalks swept, the dormitory rooms cleaned not by students as they were in Cameroon, but by a large staff of friendly people—white people, themselves so prosperous that they drove to work in cars. The buildings—made of brick in the colonial style, 100 years old and more—were immaculate. The administrators were kind, helpful, generous; the faculty were eager to see every student succeed. In sum, the America I found on setting foot upon its shores was more than equal to the dreams that I had had of it.

Americans who have lived abroad will have observed the strangeness that comes of finding on their return that much at home has changed. The country is so dynamic that even those who live here sometimes have difficulty accepting it. Buildings rise where others some weeks past had stood. Fashions come and go at each quarter of the calendar. The places one knew as a child have often been obliterated, so that a man might get lost in streets he'd once walked every day for years. In Cameroon by contrast change comes—when it comes at all—very slowly.

And yet the swiftness of the change which sweeps each day across America, of which those returning from a time abroad have an inkling, is nothing compared to the shock that confronts a third-world immigrant. No images from television can prepare a new-comer for the marvels of a place where drinking water runs even from sprinklers onto lawns; where clapboard houses are so well maintained that some are painted every other year; where the windows of the shops are washed each day; where machines sweep urban streets once or twice a week, and the gasoline, cheap by the standards even of Europe or Japan, runs from pumps that never empty.

In my first weeks at Westbrook College I walked about in a haze of awe and disbelief. The girls in my classes wore skirts so short that at first I was embarrassed. Students called their profes-sors by their first names—unheard of, beyond imagination at Yaoundé University. Supermarkets, enormous and stunning, of-fered aisles of fruits and vegetables, of canned goods and fresh meats, of products with which to clean one's house that seemed to run for miles.

The new sights were unexpected, often, even, shocking. I re-member one day in particular, not long after my arrival, when to my surprise as I walked down an aisle in one of the college's administrative offices, a machine began typing by itself. It was, as I soon learned, a printer, to which a message had been sent from the terminal of some distant secretary. To me though, it was the machine itself performing a task which had theretofore, so far as I knew, required a human being. I was shocked and, soon enough, afraid, for as my mind worked to understand how such a thing was possible the only answer that came to me was that it must be some kind of ghost or other spirit. In my fright I jumped and turned, and with pleading eyes sought the aid of the administrators who had been walking me through the paperwork of matriculation.

It did not take long, I hasten to add, before the wonders of such futuristic technologies began to draw me towards them in a kind of ecstatic joy. Computers were an invention more brilliant than any I could ever have imagined, for I had never heard of a type-writer on which one might type without having to move a carriage at the end of each line. In the pleasant well-lit computer center, such miraculous machines stood rank and file—a score of them or more. Each was occupied by an earnest student whose focus on the screen seemed to me complete, an idea that thrilled me. The only sound that could be heard was of clicking keys tapped by furious, expert fingers at speeds that astonished me. Like an insect to a lamp I was pulled to the computer by the same power which had drawn me to the cars, the planes, the helicopter.

The director of the center sat me down at one of the terminals. A student-assistant perched beside me. The little box that flick-ered on the screen was called a cursor. At the end of one line another line appeared spontaneously. I was surprised to find the arrangement of the keys on this machine exactly like those that I had known at home, and with a kind of smug pride I too was soon clicking with abandon. I might never have stopped, I think, if some appointment had not pulled me away. There was no end to the lines I might type, I thought. I might sit here for the rest of my life—for eternity, even—and still when I sat back the cursor would be flickering, awaiting my command.

Even as I grew familiar with the workings of the computer, I could not help continuing to be impressed by the focus of the students around me as they peered into their screens. At Yaoundé University distractions abounded everywhere one went, for the students were a rowdy crowd, many of them indifferent to their educations. Here in the Computer Center, though, I found a joyous quiet.

The possibility that one might study with an eye not to the job for which such knowledge was essential, but for its own sake, was, I think, among the loveliest of all those things which I discovered. Philosophy, history, the poetry of Shelley—these were read for the ideas they contained, not for the advantage they might give one in the marketplace. So too as the idea of a liberal education dawned on me, did I appreciate the time I had for contemplation.

My luck in finding my way to Westbrook College struck me especially one day when I ventured through the line of trees that separated its campus from a large cemetery, the likes of which I'd never heard. It's still there, and will be there when I myself am dust beneath a stone. Its name is Evergreen, and it happens, as I learned, to be one among a handful of the park-like resting places laid out in the 19th century in the so-called garden cemetery movement. Like the first such cemetery to be built in this country—Mt. Auburn in Cambridge, Massachusetts—Evergreen spreads out endlessly, across 240 acres of freshly mown grass, rustic paths, and moss-covered gravestones, to the edge of a woods that appeared limitless to me. Stands of spruce trees, planted as saplings with a thought to their growth through the centuries, give the place its character. Pines and firs, maple, oak, and elm trees had also been cunningly placed not just to shade but to be appreciated for themselves. At Evergreen Cemetery, obelisks reach to the clouds. Mausoleums larger than my mother's house rise atop pretty, grassy knolls. Every road and path possesses a name and a street sign to go with it, so that visitors won't lose their way.

From an apprehension left over from my feelings for the burial grounds of Kom, I did not visit Evergreen until some days after my arrival. At home as I well knew evil spirits liked nowhere more to live than in graveyards with the bones that they have left behind. When forced by circumstance to walk past one of these terrifying places, I walked quickly, with hurried steps and eyes cast anywhere but towards the stones or wooden crosses marking graves, for fear of rousing the ire of ghosts that lurked thereabouts.

Someone, though, on my second or third day at school, had spoken fondly of the beauty and the peacefulness of Evergreen, and urged me to see it for myself.

In time, as my curiosity overcame my fear, I went. Groups of students, having found the freedom of the place, sat or lay about, singly or in groups of twos and threes, their heads in books or chatting in the hushed tones that seemed to indicate a kind of reverence for the people buried there. To a man and woman they looked at me and smiled, for as one of only three black-skinned students at the college I was known to everyone. These restful-seeming students and the comfort rather than the fear that their surroundings had evoked were reassuring. The beauty of Evergreen, once I had grown accustomed to the idea of walking across the bodies of the dead, could not help drawing me further into it.

Here and there I observed the little flags that had been described to me, and which indicated the graves of veterans who had served in one or another of the country's wars. Some of the stones beside these flags gave the soldiers' dates of service. The idea of sacrifice for a single nation does not exist in Cameroon. At last count some 260 tribes inhabit the country, whose history as a colony—first of the Germans, and then of the French and English—has had no real unifying idea. I'm sure that most people in Cameroon could not name a single leader of its war of independence against the French throughout the 1960's.

Standing beside these graves I recalled those who had sacrificed—if not their lives, then at least the comforts of their homes—to bring education and Western medicine to Kom. For all I knew missionaries and Peace Corps volunteers of the sort who had had such a profound effect on me were buried here. The engineers who had given us the Belo Water Project, the men and women who had built the aero-planes, the cars and trucks, the television sets—they or their kind might be lying just beneath my feet. At that moment I could not help thinking how lucky I was that some small part of their sacrifice had been made for me alone, to keep me healthy, to inspire me with their miraculous inventions, to bring me to this lovely place.

To me, who had dreamed of coming to America since the age of twelve, the idea of such sacrifice was further evidence of the goodness of the place. In time I would learn that the abundance of America which had astonished me on my arrival was not shared equally; that a poverty no less ugly than that I'd known in Cameroon does exist; that drug abuse such as isn't known in my country has sent thousands to the gutters here. But at that moment, in that place, beneath the waving branches of the spruces and the unfamiliar songs of birds whose names I'd not yet learned, I knew that America was exactly the place of which I'd dreamt so long, and that I could sigh in the relief of having reached my journey's end.

CHAPTER SIXTEEN

A third-world immigrant's arrival in a country like America is a curious experience. Though I was at first disoriented, what strikes me on recalling those days so many years later is how soon all that had been strange seemed commonplace; how incredible is the power of human beings to adapt to new environments. That white people with cars should be cleaning my toilet, which at first struck me as bizarre, began within a week or two to seem the natural order of things. I who had so often scrubbed clothes in backyards from a bucket, who had never seen or heard of machines that did the task, or of powdered soap in little boxes, was soon plugging quarters into the machines in our dormitory basement as if I'd done it all my life.

But for a while—a few weeks, a month or two—everything was new. Every fantasy that I'd ever had of America, whether generated by the media or by the technology that Americans produced or by the Americans I'd known or seen, was replaced by the new reality. Every meal taken, every step walked on unfamiliar pavement, every item in every store was new. The species of the trees had never been imagined. The flowers that grew in every flower bed were flowers I had never seen or touched or smelled. I went to the ocean. It smelled vastly different from the ocean in my native land. People moved their bodies differently. Girls wore bikinis at the beach. Dogs lived with people in their houses—Dogs! Which in Mamfe had been served as food!

Among those things that most astonished me was how far even strangers would go to help a new arrival. I was during those first few weeks of school without money, for my lost luggage had held my travelers checks as well as all my clothes. But though American Express would soon transmute my lost dollars into cash, the clothes were another matter—a circumstance which led me to observe first-hand the generosity of Americans for their fellows, which, in Cameroon, is reserved for family alone. It seemed strange to me that the college's Director of International Affairs should take a personal interest in the welfare of a single student, and yet he did. I will never forget the man. His name was Don Bouchard. He took me to a department store to buy a few essential items with money that he loaned me from his pocket. He took me on a tour of Portland. He arranged for the local paper to interview me—for such an immigrant as I was an exotic then in small-town America.

The students too—students whom I had never met—brought clothes and toiletries from home, which they gladly pressed on me. Again and again a friend of mine, a Japanese named Masami who owned a car, carried me back and forth between our campus and the airport as I struggled unsuccessfully to recover the suitcase that was lost.

I understood at once on my arrival that I was to be a celebrity at Westbrook College, when, stepping from the taxi that had carried me from the airport, I was greeted by a group of students who happened to be standing there. These students were certain that I must be the African whose trip from Cameroon had carried him by way of Colorado. They knew my name. They inquired of my health. They took me to the college office. And it was not just on my arrival that I was treated as someone special: for the rest of my time at Westbrook I was greeted wherever I went with nothing but smiles and warm regard.

I had a roommate for a while until the surfeit of empty dormitory rooms allowed me to take one for myself. The roommate came from India—a bright but lazy guy who slept all day and eventually flunked out of school, and who had hung on the wall above his bed a poster of a sexy Indian starlet. This poster aroused the imitative nature of my soul, so that I'd soon bought posters of my own, and thereafter slept beneath the images of Cindy Crawford and Madonna.

One Sunday a week or two following my arrival I went to church—the eighth such place of worship I'd ever entered, I believe, and, excepting the Belo Church, perhaps the most significant. It's called the Central Square Baptist Church—a pretty structure built of stone in 1907, with steeply sloping roofs of slate and a bell tower topped by a dome.

On my first visit to the church one Sunday not long after my arrival, the congregation turned as one to look at me. On every face I saw a smile of welcome for this newcomer to their sanctuary—an African, the only black-skinned person in the place—as if they'd been expecting me. In a way, I guess, they had, for their door was open to anyone who wished to come inside. An usher took me to my seat. I thought the service beautiful. And though I don't remember what message was preached that day I recall thinking that it was not only inspiring, but that it was being spoken for my benefit, as if the pastor, Calvin Hayes, had written it with me in mind.

Until that day I had never known a service performed without two ministers—one to speak in English, the other to translate the message into Kom; or one to speak in French, the other to inter-

pret it in English. The hymns, though familiar to me, were sung in
the peculiar accents of America. The organ was a marvel, for in
Cameroon hands were clapped and drums were beaten when we
sang.

Following the service I shook hands with the pastor and his
wife. In the fellowship hall the congregants sang "Happy Birth-
day" to all those who'd celebrated that anniversary in the past
week. Someone asked me if I wanted to join the church and I said
yes at once, and was given a card to fill out, and thus in the space
of two hours became the newest member of a large community. I
was asked to the associate minister's house for lunch. The family's
name was Sholl, who would in time become among the closest
friends that I would ever have. The atmosphere of welcome gave
me the warmest feeling of belonging. And so it seemed to me as
the Sholls drove me back to the Westbrook campus that in a way
my destiny had demanded that I come to Portland, Maine, to this
particular college, and to the Church that would be a second home
to me for years.

The fall of the first semester of my first year at Westbrook was
a magical period of my life. For the first time since the age of six I
had little work to do except to study—a work-study job consisted
of performing small office tasks for some 20 hours a week. New
sights, new ideas, new friends filled my life. At moments now and
then, especially sitting on a campus bench that I had come to
frequent, I'd pause and shake my head at my good fortune. How
lucky I was, I often thought, to have found myself by accident at
this obscure little college in an obscure little town in a state that I
would learn is the third most rural in America.

The bench where I often sat became a special place for me, not
unlike the granite outcropping in Fundong with its splendid
mountain views. This bench, instead of looking out across a valley,
gave the equally lovely prospect of redbrick Georgian buildings,

grassy lawns crisscrossed by walks, enormous maples, oaks, and evergreens. It was on that park bench where I read the first letter I received from my mother. She had been distressed, she said (through the scribe who had translated and written it for her), to hear of the ill fortune of my trip, my flight to Colorado, the loss of all my luggage. For the price of a chicken, though, as my mother hastened to reassure me, she had received from a soothsayer the word that things would all work out.

I began to visit the bench as often as I could. That fall of my first semester was what I would learn to call an Indian summer, with a warm sun, deep blue skies, the bright red and yellow leaves for which the area is famous—which all could be contemplated in a way that is only possible when we are present in the world. On that bench I could think about my day. On it I could work out problems great and small. In time I came to feel that it had been placed there for me as a kind of pew from whose vantage I could appreciate all that God had made. The school buildings that I loved, the trees and grass whose shadows stood in such relief beneath a hot New England sun—these were all gifts which I must treasure. I prayed there and thanked God for my good fortune, for the gifts that He had given me. Again and again I was reminded that no matter where my life should take me I would never be alone.

I would soon find God a more than welcome companion as the branches of the maple trees grew bare, and the Indian summer's cloudless skies gave way to darker days. My life, like anyone's, was not without those sorts of problems for which one might ask God for help in solving, but for which God has also given us the responsibility of seeking to resolve ourselves. There were at the time two such worries, which, like a jigger in one's foot, first irritated and then began to plague me with the pain they caused.

The first of these concerned money.

I had brought from Cameroon on the trip to America some $1,500 of the savings from my job in Fundong to cover tuition, room, and board for my first semester at the college. The rest I had left with my brother Timothy to transmit to me as needed. What I hadn't counted on was that the political turmoil beginning in my native country as I left grew worse; that protesters would rise to speak against Paul Biya, the country's head of state, in a cause that was as futile as it was just; that the country's currency would be suddenly devalued; and that, in short, I would soon be penniless. Like many people in such cases, I suppose, I refused for a while to acknowledge this circumstance, trying, and failing, to imagine that a problem put from mind might by some good fortune disappear from reality as well.

The second issue that nagged me concerned my grades, and the difficulty generally of adapting to an alien system of education. In Cameroon I had through hard work found that I was the equal of any task which my schoolwork placed before me. In America I found that no amount of work could stop me from failing. With written essays I had little trouble, for my English was better than the administration had calculated it would be. The math, the science, the economics courses though, all bedeviled me. There were, I know, large gaps in the knowledge that these classes required as prerequisites, but what strikes me most in retrospect at least is that the tests themselves were so different from anything I'd known before.

It's nearly unimaginable for those who have been weaned on examinations by multiple choice to comprehend the hours of experience that are required to master them. At the college level the questions on such tests contain a complexity that isn't superficially apparent. It takes time to learn to read the questions carefully for nuanced distinctions, and to understand that answers abound which are solutions to a wrong track one has taken. Whatever the causes, though, there was no question by the middle of my first semester that with grades of 45%—grades which, in fact, in Cameroon would have been acceptable—I was failing badly.

By Christmas I found that I had failed every subject except English and that my grade point average stood at 1.4. With the sympathy that I have found typical of such institutions in Maine, the administration informed me that tutors would be assigned to me. The truth of it, though, as they explained, was that no student at Westbrook had ever graduated whose GPA had sunk so low as mine. I was placed on academic probation.

It was with a mixture of fear and happy expectation, then, at Christmastime, that I arrived at the house of a widow named Avis Mitchell—who had welcomed me at Thanksgiving as well—to spend the holiday. With my failing grades and dim prospects of succeeding in school, and my inability to pay for my education even if I did, the fear grew in me that I might find myself on an airplane once again, this time heading east to Cameroon and to a failure which I would not forget. My hostess, though, was the sort who could banish for a time the direst thoughts, and I can think of few ways I might have better spent Christmas day than with Avis and her family.

I was not prepared for the significance which Americans attach to the holiday—for the Christmas tree, the music, the presents and the air of good wishes and conviviality. In Cameroon though I had known that the date of December 25th marked the birth of Christ, we did not take much notice of the day. What memories I have of childhood Christmases are hazy. I recall that my mother gave us an extra bowl of rice, a nice stew, perhaps, and that we walked about the village visiting friends and relatives. We did not exchange gifts, though. Nor did we hear any sort of special sermon in Belo as we did at the Scarborough Free Baptist Church where Avis took me to a service. For this Christmas Eve service, we participated in Christmas plays depicting the coming of angel Gabriel, announcing the actual birth of Christ. It was insightful and inspiring. We were provided with new clothes only at Christmas. I think Christmas meant a lot to me in Belo once I became a Christian. There were no nativity scenes or caroling in the comunity as at the Scarborough Free Baptist.

Around the Christmas tree at Avis Mitchell's house, beside a fire, with a cup of eggnog in my hand, I forgot my worries for a time. I reflected on my blessings. I found comfort in the knowledge that God had had a son who died for me, and that the two of them were never far away. Instead of contemplating all the things I lacked, I gave thanks for all I had.

I like to think of God. I like to think of Jesus too, who in my mind even now resembles the Jesus whose picture appeared on a page of the tatty flip chart in my elementary school. In the trees, in the flowers, in the snow that covers the earth in wintertime in Maine, I see them both. They are omniscient, omnipotent. I speak to them in many ways—when I read the Bible; when I pray; when I sing the hymns in church. I feel in their presence that I myself am looking down upon the earth and more able than at other times to appreciate its wonders. I feel the way one might feel after awaking from a long sleep to see each flower bud and drop of rain as something astonishing and beautiful. I'm not perfect, I know. No one in this world can be. Everyone stumbles. Everyone errs. No, I think, I am a sinner. But from prayer, from remorse, regret, apology, I know too that all my sins might be washed away and that in God's eyes for a while at least I'll be innocent again.

CHAPTER SEVENTEEN

Indeed, no matter what adversity life has brought to me—and I have suffered worse calamities than failing grades and the fear of deportation—I've found that hard work and prayer help me overcome it. In the second semester of my freshman year at Westbrook I was supplied by the administration with a tutor each for my mathematics and economics classes. They were both women, juniors or seniors I believe, one from India and one from somewhere in the States. With their help I caught up with the requirements necessary for my studies. Understanding how to take multiple choice tests was a problem that I solved myself.

The struggles with money were another matter. I would be kicked out of school if I could not pay my tuition. And though I was able with the help of Avis Mitchell's daughter Elaine to get a job off campus, I could only work so much. I could not take fewer courses, for as a condition of my visa I was required to enroll as a full-time student. In desperation I sought the counsel of my fellows at the Central Square Baptist Church, where I had come in four short months to feel at home. Through them my prayers for relief were answered: the Church intervened on my behalf with the college administration, and that semester bore the full cost of my tuition. What can one say of such kindnesses? How can one ever give sufficient thanks for the sacrifices made on one's behalf? We try. I have spoken my thanks many times to those who helped me during those bleak winter months in Maine when my future hung precariously. Still, I cannot help thinking that thanks are small recompense for sacrifice.

I liked the job I took serving hamburgers at McDonald's. Again as during those first few months at Westbrook College everything about the place surprised me. We did not have fast-food restaurants in Cameroon. We did not take seriously the idea of coming punctually to work, or have time-cards that one must punch into a clock. We did not get paid on time. I had never heard of a cheese-burger or an Egg McMuffin, of a dishwasher, an ice machine, a freezer that one entered through a door. In fact the first time I was told to fetch something from the freezer I was shocked to find that the door had closed behind me. I pushed on it—not hard enough as I learned —and when it didn't open I grew frightened. I pounded on the door. Soon enough my beating fists were heard, and when I was released I laughed with all the others at the mistake that I had made.

The store manager praised me for my dependability and hard work. It wasn't hard to be a model of the fast-food employee— courteous, efficient, and well-groomed. My colleagues for the most part lacked education and ambition. They came and went in such numbers that within a few months I'd earned the benefits of seniority. Indeed, I watched the arcs of their careers with fascination. Some were quick to learn; others slow. A great many I thought very strange, and often wondered where they lived, with whom, and how. They came, they went, stopping for a month or two and vanishing.

I have sometimes reflected that my concept of work differs substantially from the idea that most people in this country have. Few Americans after all subsist on that food which their labor alone brings to their tables. I don't mean that Americans aren't hard working—they are. Indeed, they have an ethic of work as something that one must do not just to live but as a duty, a kind of moral obligation which one owes as much to society as to oneself. It's an ethic I admire so much that I found in time I'd adopted it myself.

Nor can I deny that for many in this country their work is long and brutal, and without much hope of bringing any more food to their tables than my mother brought to ours. And yet small hope is not the same as no hope, for in Cameroon without a sponsor like Pa Andrew there truly is no future. In Cameroon, education is a luxury. Here it is provided free by law even to the children of illegal immigrants. In a world where one's horizon lies no further than the end of the field that he is tilling, work is accepted as a part of life no different than the breathing of the air. Work is not a concept to be contemplated. It produces nothing like satisfaction. And though one enjoys it no more than anyone in a country as rich as the United States, there is a kind of peace of mind that comes of its acceptance. As one eats, as one sleeps, as one in time grows old, so too does he plant the seeds and pull the weeds and at season's end pick the corn and flay the rice.

From the hours I put in to work and study, I had little time for recreation or for the friendships that one makes as a result of it. What friends I had came from my church. What friends I had from church were for the most part casual: I enjoyed their company in the parish hall, at church picnics and at other outings, but with the exception of a single family I grew intimate with none of them. And yet if I can count as my intimate acquaintances the members of a single family, it's also true that they have been more than enough to fill that space in our lives which so demands close friendship.

Their name is Sholl. They are the family that invited me to lunch on the Sunday that I made my first appearance at their church, and who afterwards drove me back to my college dormitory. They are the family with whom I have spent most of my holidays; whose children became like siblings to me; whose grandchildren are by any measure except blood my rightful nieces and nephews.

Doug Sholl was at that time the associate pastor at the church. Betsy is a poet who teaches at the university level and was once the poet laureate of Maine. I shared for a time a room with their son, Matthew, forgoing Madonna and Cindy Crawford to sleep beneath the icy stare of Mel Gibson and Danny Glover's knowing look. I have looked after their house when they traveled abroad. I have gone to them time and time again for advice and consolation. I have laughed with them and cried with them. They have taken me places in both the literal and figurative senses that I would never otherwise have seen.

It was Betsy who first showed me a side of America that I had not imagined. Soon after I met the Sholls, Betsy mentioned that she volunteered once or twice a week at one of Portland's soup kitchens. When I inquired what a soup kitchen was, and she explained, I could not despite my knowledge of her character and honesty quite accept what she had said. There were people in America without houses, without work, without the means to feed themselves? Indeed there were, as I learned first-hand when Betsy took me there one day to help serve the homeless lunch. I was astonished to see that people here could look so terrible; that so many walked the country's streets who had not bathed in months;

that a place of such vast riches should let the mentally ill fend for themselves. Even in Cameroon such people are cared for—not by the state, to be sure, but by their families.

Had I not seen the homeless for myself I would never have believed they could exist. Nor am I alone in the world in having had this disbelief, for the concept of poverty in America is not one that most third-world people can imagine. No images of the poor, the ill, the drug-addicted in America reach the vast majority of the peoples on this earth, who know almost to a man and woman that if only somehow they can reach America their dreams will be answered, their troubles magically resolved.

It's revealing of the Sholls that from their friendship my first experience with the homeless in America should have been one of helping rather than of gaping at them from the window of a car. It's true that we make our lives ourselves, but it's just as true that others help to make us who we are. From my long friendship with the Sholls I'm better able to remind myself to practice what I preach. I'm better able to find courage in hard times. At Christmastime after Doug has blessed our bread it is the family's habit to go around the dinner table beginning with the youngest for each to speak of the highest and the lowest moments of the year. It's something I look forward to. I always think while I'm reflecting on my past how glad I am to have such friends.

As I have come to love the Sholls so too have I come to love my adopted home in Maine, which has welcomed one who at first was so exotic that people asked to touch my hair. Even today, as a great many Africans have since immigrated here, I feel like something of a special person. In the 1980s I was a great deal more than that—a celebrity who was known to everyone on my campus and asked to speak to children in elementary school, some of whom, I think, had never seen a black-skinned person. Such celebrity has made me feel that I've had an impact on people's lives. I am an ambassador. People have many times invited me into their homes not just from generosity but to learn something of a culture that had seemed unknowable to them.

Beyond my studies and my work, beyond my church and those whom church had led me to and the places they had taken me, my college years were otherwise unremarkable. I learned to ride a bike—a bike that Doug Sholl gave me as a present—in the cemetery beside our campus lawns, falling time and time again and feeling a great fool. I learned to drive a car as well, a comical experience beside which my efforts with the bicycle paled. I signed up with the Vance Driving School. Some of my classmates were as young as fifteen years old, most were not much older. I was ancient by comparison. And when, in time, with the classroom work completed, I sat behind the wheel of an automobile for the first time in my life, I turned to my instructor.

"Where are the brakes?" I asked.

This question hung upon an air of disbelief. The eyes of my fellow students grew wide, for I suppose they thought that I was going to crash the car and kill them all at once.

Even the instructor, a confident man with a reassuring presence, was startled to think that an adult might walk this earth for whom the location of a car's brakes was a mystery to be unlocked.

At once he and the two students sitting in the back exclaimed.

"On the floor, Richard!"

The instructor pumped his own brake up and down to make sure that it was functional.

With the sixteen-year-olds, though, I did learn the mechanics of the automobile, the technique of merging onto freeways, the imperative of looking both ways at intersections. I passed my test, and soon enough had entered the ranks of drivers, who were to me the only true Americans.

In the spring of 1991 I received from Westbrook College my diploma.

When I marched out to take the certificate from our president, a cheer erupted. Whoops filled the air, and the sounds of endless clapping. Everybody on the campus knew my story, and understood what a long and difficult path I'd taken to that place. The moment I flipped the tassel of my mortarboard from the left side to the right was one of the best of my life, and could have only wished one thing more: that my mother whose determination had made it possible could have been there to witness the event.

CHAPTER EIGHTEEN

Upon graduation from college the world is at one's fingertips. The path of life that stretches out ahead is a Yellow Brick Road whose end must lie in the riches, the good health, and the fulfillment that compose one's private Oz. How could one not achieve success feeling as one does at that moment in one's life? How could a Kom not imagine that however winding his python trail, however many hills scaled and rivers forded and rocks stumbled over, that the way had not at last been cleared?

It's not true of course, as we all learn in time. And yet how sweet is the taste of boundless possibility, how lucky one is to have felt that way at all!

Upon my graduation I took my first apartment—a room really, in a bed and breakfast that doubled as lodging for more permanent guests. I remember only one of the other tenants, a student at the University of Southern Maine named Richard Rombalski. We often cooked together—dreadful, unhealthy food, I remember: spaghetti with sauce from a jar; frozen dinners; chicken wings by the gross. With the help of the Westbrook College Career Center I had like other seniors during my last year in college begun to develop a resume. Like these same students I found as well that doors to the world of commerce which I had imagined to be open wide were mostly closed to me.

While I looked for work worthy of my education I took a job that Doug Sholl found for me as a delivery man at a place called Country Farm Furniture Store. It was run by a conservative Christian man, who attended a prayer meeting each morning before work and carried with him at all times a copy of the Bible. It was a distasteful job. The work was mean, unchallenging, physically demanding. My coworkers lacked any education beyond the high school level and for some reason took a dislike to me. As I soon discovered, they found every opportunity to disparage my work to our Bible-toting boss. The most malicious of these young men—I don't recall his name—was a skinny guy who one day called me a nigger to my face.

There was though from taking the job at the Country Farm one benefit. In order to get from my apartment to work, a trip of 25 minutes by car, I needed transportation. The only means of transportation available between these two points, besides my feet and legs, was an automobile. I had saved $2,500. And so it was one day that with the help of a Mr. Perkins from my church, that I became the owner of a 1976 Plymouth Valiant—a sporty little four-door, yellow, with a black top. In Cameroon only the rich own cars, and so, to me at least, and to my friends and relations at home, this acquisition raised my status there immeasurably.

Oh, was I proud of that car! For months I drove around Portland with the window rolled down and my elbow resting on the door just like the men in Belo whom I had so envied so many years ago. In Cameroon the roads were made of dirt, full of ruts and holes, and so muddy in the rainy season as to be nearly impassable. In America the roads were paved. Up and down the streets I drove with no other object than to smile at people and wave to them as if the whole world were my neighborhood and everybody in it were my friend.

The joys given me by my new car, however, were insufficient to overcome my dislike of the job at the furniture store and my failure despite continued effort to secure any sort of meaningful work. I thus began to consider that graduate school would be my only avenue to a job commensurate with my abilities, and so with the idea of applying to schools of public administration, I took the Graduate Record Examination. In a way, this effort was in retrospect much like my preparation for college four years earlier. I was excited. I was eager. And yet now, just as in the first semester of my freshman year, I was shocked to learn that my scores when they returned were dismal—too dismal, in fact, as I was told, to gain my acceptance at any program in the country.

With that in mind I resolved to hire a tutor at $9.00 an hour—a large sum in those days, coming from the pocket of a furniture delivery-man—to take me through the test. He was a Chinese student at the University of Southern Maine who was said to have gotten a perfect score on that exam. With his help my own score improved enormously. And yet, because of the policy at that time of requiring all assessments to be sent into the testing service, even this score was barely good enough to make a difference. It was only through the persistence of Tom Taylor, a faculty member at the University of Maine at Orono, who had made it a mission to recruit black students to the program, that I was accepted conditionally. And so it was with his assistance that I set off in the fall for my first long trip in the Valiant, to the school where I would spend the next two years of my life.

I came to roost in a suburb of Bangor not far from the university with a family named Smith. Their house lay at a place on the Penobscot River, which dams have turned into a lake. I had never lived beside a body of water, and wondered aloud if hard rains might not raise its level so that my basement room would fill with water. The Smiths assured me that the dam had been placed there to prevent such flooding, and that of all the concerns I might have on moving in, this need not be one of them. And so I settled into my room, and to the pleasant meals I often shared with them, into the rituals of driving on Sunday mornings to their church—in short into a place within their family.

It's curious to me looking back on my two years in graduate school that the academics themselves seem to have played a smaller role in my education than my experience outside the classroom. Despite my conditional acceptance I did well in school. The classes weren't difficult. I learned a great deal about public administration and finished two years after my arrival with a grade-point average of 3.5.

In Orono I had a Jamaican girlfriend, Grace, tall and lithe and beautiful, who was in the second year of an MBA program. I joined organizations by the handful—the African American Students Association, the Organization of International Students, the Campus Crusade for Christ. I volunteered for service projects at the Smith's church, and found work stocking supermarket shelves.

Of all the organizations I joined in my first year at UMO, and of all the activities I participated in, it was the African American Student Association that had the greatest impact on my life. It was run by a black woman, Cheryl Daley, who was the head of the university's multicultural program. She was a woman of medium build but large personality, with an afro just beginning to go gray, whom I never saw dressed in anything but pants. She was always smiling. I will never forget her, and all she did for me, and I'll be grateful to her for the rest of my life.

The University's African American Association was at that time filled with student athletes who came from places like Chicago's South Side, which, in my imagination anyhow, were dangerous, exotic, and intriguing, in the way that places with an air of menace cannot help being. These men and women were sophisticated in ways that I was not. I thought them very cool, but, also, difficult to understand, for their English was not like any other I had heard. Indeed so foreign was their dialect that I was impressed almost to the point of astonishment that Cheryl Daly could move as easily between it and standard English as a linguist might move from Ancient Greek to Dutch.

The African Americans puzzled me in other ways as well, for it seemed to me as if they carried about them a chip on their shoulders, seeing prejudice behind every rock and corner, where it did not always exist. And yet incidents of prejudice were commonplace enough that I couldn't really blame them. It was Cheryl's job through our Association to monitor such incidents, whether subtle or overt. Each week when we met, Cheryl would inquire whether anyone had had issues which might have resulted from the color of our skin. There always were.

Though I know it to be true that others see me as an African, I have never thought of myself as black. This is among the differences in outlook that most distinguishes we who were born in Africa from Americans of African descent. In a world where everyone is the same color, one doesn't notice color. In a world of people with skin of many different colors—and especially in a country with a such a history as America's—its people pay attention to such things.

My experience with the Black Students' Association was my introduction to racism here. I was astonished recently to hear that President Obama—a light-skinned, upper-middle class, well-dressed man—had himself heard doors lock as he walked across the street in front of waiting cars. It takes time to become attuned to such small things—not just to have an ear to hear the quiet locking of the car, but the history to know what it means. Often people have to tell you these things. Dark-skinned people, Jews, and others hear the stories from their parents at an early age. The signs are taught like the ABC's. Now I too began to see racism where I had not seen it before.

I needed other work as well, and so, for the job of cooking hamburgers I applied to a campus restaurant called the Bear's Den. But though the job did not seem especially demanding—I had experience at that work after all—I was puzzled when my application was turned down. Without Cheryl Daly, it would never have occurred to me that this was anything but one more of life's many disappointments. With Cheryl to show me—and with her influence—I was soon flipping burgers at the place.

Now too I began to see racism in the attitude of—of all things—a black man, the Assistant Director of Admissions, who seemed to treat me differently than he treated the whites he supervised, berating me for the smallest offenses and presuming to give me grades on my performance though he had no authority in the matter. He was an angry, bitter man, with an afro and a mustache going gray. I detested the man, and I was not alone. From time to time he disappeared without word of where to find him. He was later fired for some infraction of the rules, and, when he sued the school for his dismissal, I was called to testify against him. I would have done so gladly, and was not a little disappointed when the case was settled out of court.

The weeks, the months in graduate school seem in retrospect a fleeting moment in my life—brief, sweet, without the complications that the real world imposes. I worked. I studied. In the springtime I sometimes dribbled my soccer ball on the grassy verge of the lake across the street. And though Grace had graduated at the end of my first year there and left, I didn't miss her much. The women in my life have come and gone, for one reason or another, without having touched me deeply in the way that love is often described. I don't know why that is.

I graduated from the School of Public Administration in the spring of 1994—happy, optimistic, unconcerned that my student visa was expiring. With the confidence bestowed by my advanced degree I felt a little like the images of Mel Gibson and Danny Glover that appeared above my bed in the room of Matthew Sholl: with the world at my fingertips, confident, armed and dangerous.

CHAPTER NINETEEN

As I write these words, some twenty years since taking my graduate degree from Orono, and looking back at the course my life has taken, I admit that I've never found that job which so much optimism had led me to believe was mine by right. I've made a living, to be sure. I do enormously satisfying work at a place called Creative Work Systems where, as a life-skills coach, I help people with cognitive deficiencies. I work part-time at a hotel. And though much time has passed, and though I have had apartments of my own, I find myself once more living with those same Sholls whose kindness, whose trust, and whose faith in me has never changed. And yet despite their love for me, despite the other joys of my life, I have suffered many hardships. I have found myself in a despair so immeasurably deep that I have thought from time to time of taking my own life by the means of drinking chlorine bleach.

I don't know whether I am cursed, or just unlucky, or whether there is something inside me that has prevented me from finding that life of which I'd dreamt so long in Cameroon—of love; of prosperity; of satisfaction taken from my work. And perhaps it's true as I've sometimes thought that the dream of getting to America, itself so urgent, so compelling that I persevered through adversities far greater than any I would encounter for many years to come—that that dream itself was not enough; that once I had arrived in America I felt as if I'd stepped upon the golden roads of fortune and that from that moment on I had nothing left to dream for.

The days, the weeks following my return to Portland passed without my getting so much as an interview. I returned to my old job at the furniture store, whose hard labor and culture of disdain worked on my nerves. The other men spoke ill of me. Months passed without the glimmer of a decent job; in time I grew despondent. It's odd to reflect so many years later on this depression which for a time defined my life.

It came on slowly at first, hardly worth noticing, but grew so large that in time it almost consumed me. After three, four, five months of looking for work without success, my dread of deportation grew.

In bed alone on those dark nights I tossed and turned. I woke up sweating, my sheets damp, my blankets in disarray. I lay awake for hours with no other thought than wondering how it was that I, who had six years of higher education, was unable to move forward; that I, who was capable of doing anything I put my mind to, could not get the job that would allow me to realize fully the American Dream I had so long sought.

"What is wrong with me?" I'd ask myself.

I felt, indeed, like the ball of string which shrinks as it's unraveled, my sense of self-worth growing smaller and smaller so that in time it couldn't help but disappear.

If the nights were bad, the days were worse. At six o'clock my little alarm clock would ring, its sound sinister, as if it were admonishing me for my failure.

"Wake up, Richard! Nothing has changed! You're still without a meaningful job! Your visa is still expired! Wake up! You're a failure! Tell me what you have to say to that!"

In the daylight hours when I was not lifting sofas in and out of trucks, I sought to remedy my plight by buying lottery tickets, singly at first, and soon enough a few every month. On occasion I traveled west to New Hampshire, which sold tickets that promised greater riches still. I did not believe, really, that I would win at these silly games of chance. I drew comfort merely from the hope they gave me.

When I was not buying tickets I was praying to God that He would help me succeed—either that or dreaming of stumbling upon some lucky break. I sought other ways to keep my misery at bay. When, in the dentist's office, I suffered injections from his dreadful needles, I embraced the pain, drawing hope of another kind, that in return for my sacrifice I'd be allowed an exit from my plight.

I wrote to celebrities, explaining my situation and asking for donations. Madonna, with whose picture I had lived during my freshman year in college, was a recipient of a missive. Oprah Winfrey got one, and Michael Jordon—there were 35 in all. And though I never received a dime from any of these figures, I did hear back from three or four of them. Shaquil O'Neal explained that he had put his efforts into helping inner-city youths. Elizabeth Taylor had turned her philanthropic focus to the cure of AIDS. Reggie Miller, the three-point wizard of the Indiana Pacers who was a favorite of mine, sent a postcard which cautioned me to stay in school and to avoid the lure of drugs.

It's true that, as with the lottery tickets, I found hope in sending off these letters. And yet however comforting was that hope, it was not enough to pay the rent and put food into my mouth. For a year or more, from the end of my optimism early in the spring of

1995 through the winter that would follow, I thought more and more of unplugging my alarm clock so that I would never have to leave the bed.

Of all the things I did in those desperate months following my graduation from Orono, among the most rewarding was to have joined the Scarborough Free Baptist Church, whose doors I first entered with Avis Mitchell at my first Thanksgiving in America. I'm still a member of the church. Among my best friends in the world are those I've met at Scarborough. They have welcomed me to Maine and given me not just the comfort of their prayers, but the money from their wallets to help me through hard times.

It was these friends I made in church—Avis Mitchell and John Nielsen especially—to whom I turned in the spring of 1996 as my fear of deportation threatened to consume me. I don't know why I hadn't done it sooner. With such good friends beside me I found that even as the threat of deportation grew more real, my fear of it diminished. I know that my friends were concerned for me. One of them—I don't remember who—telephoned the local office of the Immigration and Naturalization Service, which, in turn, urged me to present myself to them.

CHAPTER TWENTY

For those who are lucky enough to have been born in the United States, it's hard to understand how large, how powerful, how ominous the Immigration Service seems to anyone who has lived even for a short while as an illegal alien here. Its authority is absolute. Its agents acquire the aspect of spies—waiting, watching, ready to appear at any moment as if from thin air. Its judgments are swift, certain, all but irrevocable. Indeed, before my friends at church convinced me of the course I ought to take, the idea of volunteering to place myself at the mercy of the I.N.S. had never crossed my mind.

At its doors I took a breath and entered. I waited my turn in line and, soon enough, found myself sitting at the desk of an official of the U.S. government. Like the customs agent in Washington, D.C.—the first American to greet me on my arrival in the States—this man seemed to hold my fate within his hands. I'm sure he'd seen countless aliens just like me, each with a story to tell and a case to be made for remaining in this country.

For his kind he was an agreeable sort. Rather than seeking excuses to deport me, he seemed to wish to help me find a way to stay.

I told him of my education in Cameroon, of my desire to reach America, of the degrees I'd taken at Westbrook College and the University of Maine.

His ears perked up when I mentioned the politics of Cameroon.

"Tell me about that," he said.

I explained to him that over the course of the last eight years a reign of terror had overshadowed Cameroon. Protests for democracy had erupted against the regime of Paul Biya, the despot who, even as I write this book some thirty years later, continues to rule there. The English-speaking north of Cameroon—my home, in other words—had suffered the worst of Biya's ruthlessness. Demonstrations were crushed. Whole villages were emptied, so that my family and friends began to write of "ghost towns" appearing throughout the region. Thousands were killed, among them a relative of mine, Evaristus Tohji, who was shot by government security forces at a rally in Bamenda.

The man at the I.N.S. nodded sympathetically—he had known nothing of the politics of Cameroon, or heard a word of this.

No one had. The news that reaches America from my native country as I've said centers on train wrecks and natural disasters.

Indeed, I told the man, I had been so astonished by the ignorance here of conditions in Cameroon that over the last eight years I'd written regularly to Maine's congressional delegation to inform them of the latest atrocities. I explained that the Republican senator William Cohen had been the most sympathetic to my cause, and that, in fact, I had at home a trail of correspondence from his staff reporting each time the senator brought my issue to the floor.

This news seemed to please the immigration man. He nodded thoughtfully.

"Go home and get this correspondence," he said. "Come back in the morning and let me look at it."

I did.

One by one I laid the documents before him.

And when, in time, he'd looked them over, the man explained that my papers could not help but bolster an application I could make for political asylum. He had at hand a list of lawyers who might take my case for free. He named one or two of them whom he held in high esteem. So it was that I met Cynthia Arn, a tall, soft-spoken advocate who at once inspired my confidence. I think that Cynthia correctly pegged me for the overoptimistic sort whose views of problems are more of their happy resolutions than of the possibility of their tragic ends. Such cases rarely succeeded, she told me. Much research would be required to prove that my life would be at risk if I returned to Cameroon. Still, she said, my argument was not hopeless. She agreed to take my case, and, in short order, obtained for me a reprieve from deportation. And if my stay in the United States was tenuous, still, for the first time in a year, I would be here legally.

My fear of lurking agents disappeared. The nightmares, the wet sheets were banished from my house. Though the fear of deportation persisted, it did not panic me as it had mere days before. Over the course of the next year Cynthia kept in touch, from time to time informing me of the progress of my case. The news was good; the news was bad; the news at times foretold my remaining safely in America, at other times my expulsion from the land.

Nor was my fear of poverty quite so dire as it had recently appeared to me, for I took at that time a job as a baggage handler with the Greyhound Bus Company. This job hardly fit the qualifications of someone with a graduate degree. I was not without the bouts of depression that follow frustrations of that sort. At times despite such friends as those from church, I couldn't help but feel a little lonely. I ate chicken wings and frozen dinners and for entertainment read or watched TV or window-shopped.

The best moments of my life came from my communications with relatives at home. For years I had made do with speaking to my family twice a year in the sorts of too-brief conversations that a cost of $4.00 per minute would allow. I tried to help them with money orders for twenty, thirty, fifty dollars at a time. I sent over-the-counter medicines like Tylenol, which were unobtainable in cities like Bamenda and considered miracles of modern medicine.

Most of the news I got from home came in letters I received from my brother Timothy. How I savored those missives! More often than not their tone was cheerful, their news the sort that makes one smile. My brother was a good writer, with a sense for telling details that could help me to imagine life as my family was living it. I greeted the arrival of a letter with the delight of a homesick child at summer camp and planned my evening around the ritual of reading it. I never opened these letters at once, but placed them on the kitchen table and began to settle into the routine of my evenings as if no word from home had come. There on the kitchen table the letter from my brother would sit among the pile of other mail as I prepared my dinner, as I ate and washed the dishes. From time to time as I watched TV I'd glance in the direction of that letter to make certain that it hadn't vanished by a power I couldn't comprehend. I showered. I took the pile of mail to bed with me. I opened every bill and solicitation until, at last, only the letter from Timothy remained.

Even then I would not tear at once into the envelope. I studied the stamps that Timothy had licked and which bore images from home, the transit markings, the signs of abuse from the many conveyances and sorting systems that had channeled it in time to my house on Gillman Street. At last I took my letter opener and with care slit the top edge of the envelope. I removed the pages with the tenderness of a mother lifting her baby from its crib. Only then, after all this patient waiting, did I allow myself to read what news it held—and even this I did slowly, taking in the words, the sentences, the paragraphs with an eye to every nuance they contained. And then, when at last I'd read the letter through, I read it through again, once, twice, three times and more, imagining again and again the scenes that Timothy described. Nor did I cease to think of Timothy's words when I had turned off my light. In my dreams I thought of them. For weeks to come I took the letter in my hands in order to recall my family and the country of my youth.

These letters were not uniformly positive, for Timothy had inevitably to write of hardship, tragedy, and death. In some letters I heard of further repression in my native land, which, though it might help me to secure my legal residence in this country, was for my relatives a daily hell. One day Timothy wrote to say that my sister Mariam, with whom I'd lived in Fundong during my tenure as a civil servant, had died. I heard reports of my mother's failing health, until, in one letter, my brother expressed his fear she would soon follow her daughter to the grave. He wondered if I could make a visit home. My mother, he reported, begged repeatedly to see me.

I longed to go. I longed to pull my mother close—that strong, kind woman with eyes so soulful I could not help feeling that she glimpsed depths in me I'd never seen myself. With my head bent in thought I spent hours plotting how, if I should be granted asylum in the United States, I could make a trip to Cameroon. I looked up the prices of travel from America. $1,500? For I who could hardly make ends meet? No problem! I began to horde my pennies against the day I needed them. I checked and rechecked times of departures from Boston to Paris, from Paris to Douala, and imagined my mother's look as I stepped into her arms.

Throughout the fall of 1997, past Christmas and on into another year, my lawyer kept in touch with me. I grew anxious. Had a date been set for the hearing on my case? Why not? What would the courtroom be like? Would I make a good impression? What should I wear on such a day? How would I behave? Had I the courage to speak up for myself? Would it matter what I said? Would the judge look kindly on my case? Would I be granted sanctuary?

The answer to these questions had nothing of the drama I'd imagined for so long. On the day assigned to hear my case Betsy Sholl and Jim and Gail Key from the Scarborough church drove to Boston with Cynthia and me.

I was asked to state my name.

The judge expressed her dismay at the events in Cameroon, which my lawyer had laid in ordered documents before her.

She wondered if the protests in my native land were something like the marches led by Martin Luther King.

Well, yes, I said, they were.

She inquired whether my relatives were not frightened for their lives. She expressed sympathy for their plight, as if confused that there weren't more like me who wished to flee such awful times.

Within 15 minutes the affair was over.

I was astonished at my good fortune. All those years spent hiding from the law; the dread of entering the office of the I.N.S.; the cautionary words that my lawyer used to keep my hopes from soaring: all that, and in a quarter hour the judge had granted my petition for asylum with an apology that it should have taken so long to work its way through the U.S. legal system.

Cynthia and Betsy and the Keys and I jabbered happily as we drove north. At home, we celebrated. For a day or two I shrugged off my fear of deportation, and mused on the ups and downs of fortune.

And then, not a week following my day court, I began to plan the trip to Cameroon which I had so long wished to make. Though as it turned out there would be no ill consequences of this travel, still, planning such a trip so shortly after I had acquired a legal standing in America was a foolish thing to do. The papers granting my asylum after all were rather flimsy evidence of my new status. What was more, for the customs agents in Douala such documents would mark me as an opponent of the Biya government. I might have been arrested as soon as I stepped off the airplane. I might have been imprisoned. For such an impulsive act I might still be waiting there.

At the time, though, from my experience in court and with the precious document in hand, I had a confidence that knew no bounds. I was so homesick, I had waited so long for the opportunity of seeing my relations, that I never considered the imprudence of making such trip. My bank account by now held just enough to let me go. And so, with no other thought than of how happy I would be on landing in my native land, I made plans to fly home.

CHAPTER TWENTY-ONE

In October, then, I traveled to New York by bus, from there by plane to Paris, and thence to Africa, where my country spread beneath me with a lushness I had not remembered. I was surprised at first and then mortified when, as our plane descended to the chief airport of my native land, the captain announced to the entire plane, first in French, then in English, that he had a message for me from the Douala tower.

"It would appear that we have a passenger from Maine who is returning home for the first time in over ten years," he began. "The message is from his mother and it reads: 'Richard, you better have a good excuse for not writing to your little old mother for all these years!'"

The other passengers laughed in a happy chorus.

"No," the captain continued in a kindly voice, "that's not really what it says. It simply reads 'Welcome home son, we are so proud of you.'"

I had no doubt that my brother Timothy was behind it. And when in a moment my embarrassment had passed I felt extremely gratified. Timothy was always doing extraordinary things for me, just as he did for his family. He was besides my mother among my greatest friends.

In the airport as I stood in line an hour or more to clear customs I was shocked to see how impoverished the country of my birth seemed to have become. Without question Cameroon had grown poorer in my absence. From somewhere I recall having learned that the country's GNP had fallen almost 20 percent in the ten years since I'd last set foot on its soil.

Still, I know that a decade spent in a first-world country must have exaggerated my despair, even a kind of mild horror, at the state of things. Smells of urine, garbage, rotting fruit filled the air. A pandemonium prevailed. If the hawkers of trinkets and exotic leather wallets had proliferated, so had the numbers of destitute— the young girls with babies on their hips; the blind; the lame, their withered limbs prominently displayed—all with hands stretched out in search of coins. It stunned me, coming from a country which in the last ten years had prospered greatly, to understand that my people were worse off than before.

But when, in the dusky October light of Douala, I saw Timothy waiting by the curb, I found that my joy at seeing him exceeded even my enormous expectations. He'd grown. He was stronger than I imagined. His smile seemed wider than before. He was standing by the taxi that had brought him from Bamenda, and which would take us back again. With him besides the driver was a friend of his named Michael, whom Timothy had brought along to provide the strength of numbers required for a journey through dark nights in Cameroon.

On the outskirts of the city after we had stopped to eat we set off on the road that runs between Douala and Bamenda. In America such a thoroughfare would be designated as "unimproved"; in Cameroon it goes by the name of a highway. I was amused recently when I looked at Google Maps to find that the sages of the internet have allowed four hours for traveling between the points by car. I'm sure that even today the trip would take twice as long as that. In 1998 we anticipated that our driver would need 12 or 14 hours to cover the distance of 180 miles.

Checkpoints lie at intervals along the road, at each one of which the traveler will find a dozen cars or more waiting in line. The inspections at these make-shift stations are interminable. Negotiations to ascertain what sort of bribe might be required to pass are delicate. One can spend an hour or more waiting to get through—delays for which, I guess, Google cannot account. Timothy had brought along $200 worth of Cameroonian francs for the purpose of these bribes alone, a sum which I supplemented generously. I gave the money to my brother, for one must leave the car for these negotiations and the sight of my new clothes, my clean white tennis shoes, would light the eyes of these policemen. Once as I recall, though I never exited the taxi, the price of moving on increased when one policeman went beyond the call of duty in more carefully examining the car's best-dressed passenger.

The trip terrified me, for as I knew bandits hid along the road to pick off the weaker in the herd of passing cars. Enormous trucks carrying logs from the interior blew us off the track, or, if the trucks had broken down beside the road, forced us to wait our turn to pass. Pickups full of plantains or bananas overtook us on dangerous curves, raced ahead in clouds of dust, and then were met again as they struggled to climb the next steep hill. Ruts so deep that a man lying down in them might be lost from sight required a careful inching forward lest the taxi's transmission be smashed or its suspension wrecked.

Somewhere about halfway through the trip we stopped at the largest of the so-called rest areas for a respite from our travel. Here we found a dozen or more cars parked and lanterns lighting tables full of grilled bush meat, avocados, and plantains laid out on newspaper; fresh mangoes, tangerines, papaya, grapes; boiled eggs; two-foot long sections of sugar cane which, when we had started up again, we passed the time in sucking on. The diversion of these sweets hardly mattered, though. Within minutes we had tossed them out the windows of our car and resumed our watch for the bandits, for the wild and frightening trucks, for the cars broken down beside the road with men filling radiators, changing tires, replacing broken belts. When I close my eyes to recall that night I hardly know how I survived it.

At dawn we made our way at last into Bamenda—weary, filthy from the clouds of dust that preceded us at every mile, desperate to reach the journey's end. Even at that early hour people by the score milled about the town: walking, sitting by the road, leaning against one dilapidated structure or another. I suppose that they were homeless to a man and woman, without work or any hope of getting it. Children seemingly alone scratched with sticks in the dust beside the rusting hulks of cars and trucks. By comparison the homeless I had seen in the soup kitchens of Portland, Maine, were less despairing by far: at least a meal awaited them each day at breakfast, lunch, and dinnertime.

At last we stopped beside the house which Timothy had built with my assistance. It was a large place for the neighborhood, a stucco affair that my brother had improved with the addition of a separate kitchen. When our taxi stopped we could see the whole family gathered, either standing by the house or sitting on a bench that stood just next to it. They weren't expecting us at that early hour, for as long as the trip from Douala had taken it should have taken longer still. They stood watching, curious to see who might emerge from the taxi. And when at last I stepped from the car, and the family had spotted me, I could see that my mother had been lost at the edge of the crowd and could not tell what the fuss was all about. It amused me to see that, like the time so many years ago when I led her neighbors up the Fungom Village trail, I would surprise her once again.

Like Timothy I was taller than I had been before, more confident, a man, now, though I had left a boy.

"*Mama alima!*" I cried. "Mom, it is me!"

I opened my arms and began to run to her.

She looked up but did not recognize me at first.

As I got closer her eyes grew wide. Her white teeth showed through the crowd. She perked up like a bird who's found a worm crawling through the grass, in the morning sun.

"*Gvi ajûŋ a Bobe ni mà!*" she called to me.

"Welcome my husband!"

She grabbed me tight, pulled me close, and whispered in my ear.

"Ayeah, my son, you're home!" she said.

Next she demanded that I sit down in her lap.

"But mother I am big now and you are small!"

It did not matter. With me in tow she perched on the bench and pulled me down on top of her. As best I could I tried not to crush the tiny woman. She began to sob with happiness and I cried too to feel myself wrapped up in her arms, her hands still as rough as eucalyptus bark from working, day after day, in the fields of Anjin where she now lived.

She wouldn't let me go even when I stood and the family swarmed around us. My sisters came to touch me. The children stood in awe of this famous visitor from America, of whom they'd heard so long, and who had assumed the proportions of a legend.

In time when we had gone inside the house my sister Eunice led the family in a prayer to thank God for my safe return. Afterwards we sang hymns, everybody clapping to the rhythm of those same Christian tunes that I had sung not one week since at my Baptist church in Portland. A large meal followed, and all the while the eyes of the children never strayed from me. My English, so improved over the years, astonished them I know, for in these family gatherings the official language of our province is intermixed with Kom.

One of my nephews approached me shyly afterwards.

"I want to go to America," he said.

I smiled at the young boy's enthusiasm and his confidence, which I could not have mustered at his age.

"If you want to go, then go!" I told him.

I could see him plotting out his future, which had taken on a new meaning in my presence. He grabbed my shirt and touched me, as if to make certain that he had not imagined this connection to a model for his future. But though I believed at that moment that the young man really could succeed, in honesty I have to say that he never did find his way to school. Without a mother of my own mother's determination; without a Bobe David; without a Pa Andrew to pay for the education necessary to success, success is hardly ever possible.

While I remained at Timothy's house, my relations, my friends, and total strangers came to look upon the man who had returned from America. And when in the days that followed I ventured forth to the villages recalled so fondly from my youth, I witnessed the same phenomenon. In Belo, in Fungom, in Kikfuini, Sho, and

Anjin people thronged to see the native son made good. Such greetings could not help but gratify me. One cannot help feeling a kind of joy at being celebrated, though I knew I was no hero to anyone but them.

In addition to the adulation accorded me at each turn and stop throughout my visit home, I received as well the supplications of the multitudes. From every corner of the country people had heard that a man from Belo had returned triumphant, and it seemed to me that all of them came to me for help. I learned then what it must be like to be a real celebrity, rich, well-known, to whom one might turn as I myself had turned to Oprah Winfrey to find a way out of my desperate circumstance. It pained me to turn them away, but what could I do? I did not have half the resources I would have liked to help even my own family.

If I was surprised, though, at the extent of the distress as I traveled through the country, still I had known that the poverty in Cameroon was bad enough, and that its cause lay directly at the feet of the Biya government. I cared about the place. I wanted it to work. I had often considered in what small way I myself might provide some help besides the gifts of money that I sent my family. For these reasons I had resolved before I left to visit the one man in Cameroon who more than any other offered hope to the people of the English speaking provinces.

His name was John Fru Ndi. He was—still is, in fact—an imposing, charismatic figure, who, though he had fairly won the race for president of Cameroon in 1992, had had his victory snatched away and been sent into a kind of exile. I suppose that he was lucky enough to have been allowed any freedom at all, though his presence as an "opposition figure" served Biya in his claims of democratic rule. For all of those who'd marched against the autocratic ruler, Ndi was a kind of champion, whose very image in photographs was cause for inspiration. He's a large, powerful man, well-built, muscular, who might be a twin of the American football player Jim Brown. In photographs Ndi is most often shown dressed in native costume with a fist raised in the air.

His headquarters lay on the third and highest floor of the tallest building in Bamenda. At the front desk when his secretary learned that I had traveled from America, I was led into an office filled with books and cluttered, with a commanding view of the spreading city below. We had a brief, engaging conversation. He inquired politely of my life in America and described the desperation of our people, the imploding economy, and the corruption of the government that lay at the root of all of it. I have often heard that Cameroon is among the most corrupt countries in the world, and found indeed, on looking recently, that its inhabitants view the place with such hopelessness that it ranks 144th out of the 176 nations surveyed by Transparency International. Still, despite the bleakness of the situation that Ndi described to me, despite my feelings of powerlessness, one cannot leave such a meeting without feeling a kind of inspiration, and a desire to do one's best to help.

At Timothy's house, too, we spoke of the country's situation. My friends and relatives described the horror of the massacres they'd witnessed, and showed me photographs of relatives of mine lying dead upon some table. And though those terrible times had passed they had not passed without a cost that came in mute despair.

We weren't gloomy much, though, during my trip home in those October weeks. We laughed. We sang. My mother told me how much she'd thought about me during those long years when we were apart, about her desire for me to find a wife, about her pride in my accomplishments and her deep love for me. Timothy talked about his job working in the shop, his dream of owning a shop himself one day. He and I spent a lot of time walking together, often for no other reason than to have a chance to chat.

One day, not long before my trip would end, Timothy took me to the campus of St. Paul's High School in Bamenda, in order to find a friend he wanted me to meet.

"Richard," he began in his serious way as we strolled along the road. "Mama is worried about you not having a wife and children, and we all want you to have a family too."

"Someday, Timothy," I said.

At the school we met a woman whom, as I soon learned, the family had picked out as a wife for me. This sort of thing is common in Cameroon. Marriage, and the procreation that must follow, are taken even more seriously there than they are in the United States. Families play an active role in making introductions, and often plan such surprise encounters as Timothy had planned for me to meet this girl.

Her name was Caroline. She was a tall, light-skinned woman, her hair cropped short as St. Paul's required, and dressed in her school uniform. I couldn't blame Timothy for wishing to set me up with her. She was beautiful, I thought, and though she seemed shy at first, she had a smile that was among the most infectious I have known. Timothy when he had finished with the introductions left us alone, and for an hour we talked of our pasts, our work, our dreams of the bright futures that lay ahead of us. I fell in love with Caroline, I think, right there on the grass of St. Paul's School. In the days that followed we met frequently. She took me home to meet her parents. Her parents came to visit me at Timothy's. Soon enough Caroline and I began to hold hands, and though we were never intimate there was between us an understanding that we might think of marrying one day.

Soon enough, and sadly, it was time for me to go home.

As I prepared to leave, mother told me once again what she had said when I arrived, out loud this time, for everyone to hear.

"I am so proud of you," she said. "I'm so proud of what you have done and what you will do. I will no longer ask myself '*Matimiwu*? What will become of my Richard?' I see now where you stand—tall, proud, on your own two feet. My world is full and bright because of you."

What can one reply to such an expression of faith, of love, of strength? I pulled her close to me and hugged her tightly. And though I'd leave my mother in the fear that I might never see her again, I had at least not just her blessing but her desire to see me off to a better world again.

At the airport when we reached Douala I thanked Timothy for all he'd done to make the trip as happy and fulfilling as I could have ever dared to hope.

He thanked me as well.

"For everything," he said. "For the money you send us, for the letters. We all look up to you. You are our life now, provider for us even if you are far away."

It gladdened me to think that I was such an important a figure in my family's eyes. And yet as I well knew my adopted country was hardly the Eden that my family believed. I looked rich in their eyes. I wore bright new tennis shoes and clothes that were so extravagant as to be unobtainable in Cameroon. The sums I earned at my humble jobs were large to my family and friends. I owned a car. I ate well. At my command pure water ran hot or cold in my apartment.

The struggle of life is complicated. There are no truths. In Cameroon I was wealthy; in America, poor. In Cameroon I was a celebrity; in America, I was one faceless soul among a quarter-billion. It's difficult to reconcile such contradictions. Rich, poor. Confident, uncertain. I was all of them at once. As I flew off to the

Land of Plenty from the Land of Very Little, I left behind the feeling that nothing was impossible, to return to that same truth which had greeted me before: that achieving the impossible is difficult indeed.

CHAPTER TWENTY-TWO

In the spring of 1996 I took a job as a baggage handler at the Greyhound Portland bus depot. Within a year I'd been promoted to ticket agent, and, in the spring of 2000, I became the assistant manager of the place. Until I assumed a role in the station's management, I had had no problems there of any sort. I was considered a model of employee. Everyone who worked there was my friend. Becoming a manager, though, changed my relations to my fellow employees in large and subtle ways. I imagine most people find the transition from wage earner to salaried manager a difficult and troubling one. Those Greyhound workers who had recently been friends were forced to perform what tasks I asked of them. Those passed over for the job now resented me.

Anyhow, that's when my troubles at Greyhound began. It was my job as assistant manager to make out the weekly schedule, and I soon began to hear reports of dissatisfaction with my efforts. The station manager told me that, like my fellow laborers at Country Farm, the employees at Greyhound had begun to talk behind my back. One of my friends told me that he'd heard me referred to as a nigger. Another called me a shithead to my face.

By far the most miserable employee whom I was asked to manage was a woman who often turned up in a daze, so that I could not help wondering if she was very stupid, or a drunk or other kind of addict, or whether the explanation for her behavior might lie in some combination of the three. I couldn't help disliking her. She was coarse, uneducated, always borrowing small sums of money and soliciting rides home after work. I obliged her readily enough. One day, some months after this woman came to work for us, I was astonished to learn that she had brought a suit against me for my supposed sexual abuse of her on one of these trips home. The manager was as perplexed as I that she should make such a claim. For the company, though, it was less expensive to settle with the woman than to fight the charge in court. She was bought off rather cheaply, I should say. For the accusation of abuse she took $3,000 and we saw no more of her.

Again, as with my promotion to assistant manager, consider my step up in 2003 to the top job at the depot, a job which, though it ought to have been a source of satisfaction, came at a time when the company was struggling to survive. The previous manager had earned $40,000 a year; I was asked to do the job for $30,000—only $1,000 more than I was making anyway. I thought my low salary might be due to the color of my skin, and brought a suit for discrimination. The suit went nowhere, but in the end it didn't matter much. Some months after I filed my complaint Greyhound closed its Portland station and I was out of work.

Consider the letter I received from the Internal Revenue service, the same year as my last promotion at the bus company, charging me $2,800 in back taxes. I know from my experience since then of the reputation of the I.R.S. which, in a reverse of the favor in which the Immigration Service is held, is as unimportant to illegal immigrants as it is notorious to the country's citizens. I was astonished to learn that I should be held accountable for having failed to file a tax return in any of my undergraduate years, when I was working part-time at a variety of low-paying jobs. I could not imagine how I might pay such a large sum, and feared once more the cunning reach of the I.N.S. and subsequent deportation—or, worse still, incarceration.

Consider finally the course of my relationship to Caroline, whom I had met through Timothy at her school in Bamenda. From our mutual attraction we had promised each other that we'd pursue our friendship across the vast space that lies between Cameroon and Maine. We corresponded regularly via email, I at my desk, she at an internet café. We talked by telephone as much as our pocketbooks allowed. Our romance blossomed. In time I asked her to marry me and she accepted. There followed a flurry of inquiries as to preferences, of plans to be made, of details to be considered and dispatched. I had had friends and lovers in my life, but never once a partner with whom I could work towards a goal that was among the most important of my life.

We agreed that the wedding would be held *in abstentia*—a fact which saddened me because I thought a church wedding more symbolic of the union of two people and had looked forward to walking down the aisle. But I could not afford to travel back to Cameroon. The bride price was paid to Caroline's family and preparations were made for a traditional Kom wedding. Bottles of palm wine, dishes of fufu corn, bush meat, chicken, goat were prepared and carried to her parents' house. The bride was smeared head to toe with a red dust, part of the wedding ritual, that is ground from the heart of the camwood tree. With Timothy standing in for me, Caroline and I were wedded in a government office by a judge.

I was married! At last! It made me happy to think that within the month I would have Caroline by my side. For the first time in my life I would have a partner to share my joys and sorrows;

someone for me to care for, whose tears I alone could wipe away; someone to nurse me in my illnesses; someone to touch as I fell asleep at night and to see each morning when my eyes blinked open. Caroline felt the same way, for she had been no less lonely than I.

But though the day of my wedding and the days of planning for Caroline's immigration that followed might have been among the happiest of my life, they might also have been the best days of our marriage. If either of us had known what frustration lay ahead we would have laughed at the thought of tying ourselves together in in such a way. The few weeks that we had foreseen as being the only barriers to our meeting would turn into months and the months into years. My frustration with the U.S. government would grow without bounds, for I could never have imagined when I proposed to Caroline that a legal resident of this country could not get his wife into it.

The certificate of marriage alone took a month to arrive in my mailbox from Cameroon. I ought to have understood from that delay alone the tribulations that awaited us.

Certificate in hand, I marched into the local immigration office to see what paperwork would be required.

The officer inquired as to my status.

"I'm a political asylee," I replied.

His face clouded.

"Oh," he said. "You are not yet a permanent resident?"

I admitted that I wasn't.

He explained that one must be an asylee for five years before he could apply for permanent residency.

I was dumbfounded. No one had ever told me that.

Furthermore, the officer continued to explain, once I was a permanent resident it would take another four years before I could think of bringing my wife to live with me in the United States.

I did the math.

Was it possible, I asked, that nine years would have to pass before Caroline could enter the country legally?

It was.

And though the man seemed to sympathize with me he shrugged his shoulders and shook his head. Sadly, there was nothing he could do.

I left the immigration office angry and confused. When I explained the situation to Caroline, to Timothy, to all my friends from the Scarborough church, they were in unanimous agreement that such policies were the most ridiculous they'd ever heard of.

At once we began a campaign to bring Caroline to the United States by other means. To solicit money for my cause, Doug Sholl sent out a letter that brought me $9,000—$5,000 alone from a Christian philanthropist whom I'd never met. I wrote to Maine's senators and congressmen in the hope that the same magic they'd used to make me an asylee could work to conjure up a visa for my wife. I appeared every month or two at the Portland office of Olympia Snowe, to plead my case in person. I drove to Lewiston for a fruitless meeting with members of Congressman Mike Michaud's staff.

Nor did we stop with lobbying. Indeed, the Scarborough congregation prayed for me on numerous occasions. They signed letters on my behalf. Ten of its members joined me one day in visiting the local office of the Immigration Service—an effort for which we were not only denied a hearing, but admonished for praying in the parking lot of a federal agency. On another occasion several of us met at the Nielsens' house to telephone the U.S. consulate in Yaoundé. I don't know what the phone call cost, but we did not succeed in speaking to anyone worth speaking to.

As Caroline by then was a student at Yaoundé University, it next occurred to my pastor that we might bring her here on a student visa to study at a local Bible school. Caroline sent her transcript to the appropriate U.S. government department. The pastor himself called Senator Snowe's office, which, in turn, sought an answer from the I.N.S. But no. That too was unacceptable.

Next I tried a local college, spending hours on the telephone and trooping down in person to its admissions office, whose director encouraged Caroline to apply. The college had many international students, he explained. Securing a visa shouldn't be a problem. In Cameroon therefore, her admission letter in hand, Caroline scheduled a review of her application at the U.S. Embassy. On the appointed day she arrived. Oh, they were sorry, they explained, but the Embassy staff were too busy just then to help her out. Come back in four weeks, they said. When the month had passed and she appeared once more, she was told that she must wait five weeks more. So it went, month upon month, until the college admission papers had expired.

The idea of bringing Caroline to America became in time an ordeal for everyone involved. My friends were weary. Caroline's family were growing angrier and angrier at what they perceived as my lack of dedication to the cause. She herself was hardly happy with the situation. At Yaoundé University she joined a cult-like Christian sect. I knew nothing about this group, or what might have drawn her to it other than despair, but I was horrified. So were her parents. We pled with her to leave the group. I wrote her emails explaining how harmful such associations could be and, when we could afford a conversation on the telephone, used my voice to do the same. Her parents grew disgusted. They wanted nothing more to do with her, they said. One day they threw her belongings into the street and told her never to come back.

In tears on the telephone Caroline asked me what to do. The only person whom I could think of to help her was my brother Timothy. And though it is difficult for a person in this country to understand the ties of family there, the truth is that Timothy and his wife, Anne, took my wife happily into their little house. She stayed there for two years, and in that time not only left the Christian cult, but worked as hard as anyone to make their home a happy one.

Getting Caroline into the United States was my main concern, but, like all such problems, it soon enough spawned others. I must support Caroline now, and in fairness should contribute to the expenses that Timothy and Anne incurred. With what, though? My job at the bus station paid me hardly enough to keep myself, let alone a family abroad. The lottery tickets, the letters to celebrities—none of them had made a difference. What, I asked myself time and time again, was I to do?

One day I received by email from a woman in Ivory Coast a proposition that seemed an answer to my prayers. She explained that her husband, a cabinet minister in Liberia, had been assassinated during a coup to overthrow the government. She and her son had fled the country and were fearful for their lives. She needed my help. Before her husband's death he had deposited in a vault in the United States the sum of $26 million, which he had wished to be put to a humanitarian use. Someone like me, who knew just the sort of use to which $26 million could be put, would help her tremendously.

With such a windfall I could not only bring Caroline to the United States, but do everything I had ever wanted to as well: I could bring clean water, medicine, and prosperity to my little town of Belo. I could help my mother and my brother and our family.

As the Liberian explained, the bank that held this money required a one-time payment of $6,000 to release it to an overseas account.

To me, that did not seem so large a sum when weighed against $26 million and all the good that could be done with it.

I wired the money in three installments via Western Union and awaited instructions as to how I should obtain the money.

No instructions came, of course. In response to a complaint I filed with the F.B.I.'s Portland office, I was told that I'd been scammed; that the Bureau could do nothing to help me recover the money; and that, what was more, if I did not stop communicating with the woman via email my actions could constitute a crime.

I am as I have said a too-trusting person, honest to a fault—the sort who even now finds it hard to believe that evil can dwell in the hearts of men. This fact saddens me. Mistrust is a burden whose weight I carry on my shoulders now, regretfully, like everybody else.

A too-trusting nature is one of the things that leads to abuse at the hands of the dishonest; desperation is another.

Now I was out $6,000, poorer by far than I had been before. I struggled for an answer. How, how could I support myself and my family?

To my relief, the answer soon came. I must go to the church once more—to that well of generosity that had never once run dry for me.

My friends were happy to oblige, with small sums given and no expectation of return.

The philanthropist who had written me a check for $5,000 did not stop with his generous donation. He too called his contacts in the offices of our senators. He introduced me to a friend of his—a man I'll call R.J. Blackman—who possessed the sorts of connections that I would need to leave my worries in the past. Had I problems with the I.N.S.? R.J. knew a man who worked there. Did I want a better job? R.J. knew another man who helped steer people like me to meaningful employment. These people did exist. I spoke to them on more than one occasion. And though none of these men's good intentions made the least difference in my life, still I know that R.J. had in good faith tried to help.

R.J. had faith in large supply.

He ran a business that sought to help the poor and which involved the loading and off-loading of foodstuffs and other merchandise from trucks. From gratitude to my benefactor at the church, as well as from my own inclination to generosity, I began to help R.J. in moving boxes. On weekends, in the evenings I showed up to lend my muscle to the enterprise, in return for which he listened to the story of my troubles. When we had finished R.J. would urge me to kneel with him in prayer, that God too might be enlisted in my cause.

But neither prayer nor well-intentioned introductions changed my prospects. The more time that passed the more desperate I grew, until, one day, hearing from friends at church that the immigration policies of Canada were less strict than they were here, I latched onto the idea that I might bring Caroline to North America through our neighbor to the north. This idea grew in me and like a terrier with a rag I would not let it go. If some family in Canada were to sponsor her, I thought, she would make her way if not to the United States then at least across the ocean that separated us. I could visit her. Bringing her to America from Canada would be easier, I thought, than bringing her from Cameroon.

One day I asked R.J. Blackman if he knew of any such family as that.

He considered the question. He thought the idea had merit.

But he knew of no such family.

As quickly as I'd conceived the scheme, I dropped it.

How, I asked myself again, was I to bring my wife to live with me?

With each email I received from Caroline I heard more and more of her dissatisfaction with the circumstances and her frustration with my ineffective efforts. Her parents, she told me, were distressed by my failure and had offered to let her come back to live with them.

"You are not going to America!" they told her. "Face the facts! Richard has not tried to get you here and Timothy could care less what happens. You belong with a man in Cameroon!"

From Timothy too I heard that Caroline wasn't happy. She might move out, he said. Then again she might not. As I grew more and more afraid of losing her, so too I grew more and more desperate for a solution to the problem.

The days passed slowly as they do when one feels cornered, like an animal without any avenue for escape from lurking menace.

One day I received an email from my brother telling me that Caroline had moved out. He had heard somewhere that she'd boasted of our marriage being over. The telephone at her parents' house was disconnected.

What ought I to do? I wondered. I still loved her. I wanted her to know it. I asked Timothy if he would visit her to know the truth of how she felt. She wouldn't see him. A cousin told him that he ought to come back next week. On his return the cousin was aggressive. She told him that the marriage was over because I did not take it seriously.

Soon after my friend R.J. Blackman phoned to say that he had found a solution to my problem. By an accident of fortune he had learned of a family in Canada that was looking for such an immigrant as Caroline to sponsor. He had looked into the matter, he said, and found that indeed, so far from making it difficult for people to set foot on its shores, Canada encouraged it. The country needed hardworking people. It needed nurses such as Caroline, who had trained at university.

The idea was not farfetched. It was my good friends at church who in the first place had mentioned Canada's less restrictive immigration policies.

We had to hurry, R.J. said. There were more people in the world who wished to immigrate to Canada than there were Canadians who wished to sponsor immigrants.

If I would give him $3,000 at once, he said, he would have my wife upon the continent within the month.

And so once more as I had with the woman in Ivory Coast I trusted too willingly the motives of one who claimed to be doing me a service. Unlike the scammer, though, R.J. Blackman was no stranger. I had sweated beside the man in hefting boxes for his business. On the floor of his house I had knelt with him in prayer. Who would have imagined such a man to be a fraud? Is nothing sacred? What has the world come to when one can't trust a friend?

But R.J. was a fraud. He did betray me. I called almost daily to hear reports of his progress on the matter which, he continued to assure me, was proceeding according to the strict schedule that had been set. The month passed, though, with no positive developments. Even I, who was trusting to a fault, began to grow suspicious. I confronted R.J. He grew frosty. In the tone of indignation which charlatans have long employed he told me that I was ungrateful.

In time I discovered that R.J. had never had the least intention of helping Caroline. He had not researched the immigration policies of Canada. There was no family looking for an immigrant to sponsor. My money had gone straight into his pocket—or, more probably, into the pockets of his creditors. Soon I learned that R.J.'s financial situation had for some time been precarious, and later heard that he had filed for bankruptcy not long after absconding with my money.

Here was another lesson learned hard: that even friends, even fellows of my faith who professed belief in Christian virtue—even they were not immune to the forces of dishonesty and avarice.

Still, I know, there continues to be goodness in the world. My acquaintance from the church who had donated $5,000 to my cause and who introduced me to the crook, paid me the money I had lost.

Hope of bringing Caroline to live with me had vanished with my money, though. Soon we ceased to speak. The days stretched into weeks with a sadness and regret, and with the fatalistic view of we who have come up against the law and lost.

Some months later, Caroline and I divorced.

I can laugh now when I recall my standing in the churchyard of the Belo Baptist church and, seeing the family of white Americans, having taken them for the embodiment of Jesus Christ. And yet it's also true that in spite of those Americans like R.J. Blackman who live to prey on the better part of human nature, the idea of America remains no less powerful in its way to me than the ideas of Christ. On the one hand, freedom; on the other, love. Opportunity for all, however difficult the path to opportunity might be; forgiveness for one's sins no matter how terrible they might be. Justice; faith. A second chance for those who've strayed beyond the limits of the law; redemption for all of us.

A large crowd filled the courtroom on the day that I became at last a citizen of the country whose torch and beckoning hand had urged me through hard times to help me reach her shores. It was October 10th, 2008, some two decades after my arrival here. The morning was clear, the sky blue. I had chosen to wear my pinstripe suit with a shirt and tie both of the color purple—a color I associate with happiness, reflection, and the freedom to which in a few minutes I too would be entitled. And though I was grateful to see that the pastor of my church and long-time member of the church John Nielsen had come to watch me take the oath, no people on earth besides my family at home could have made me feel happier to see that day than Betsy and Hannah Sholl.

There was nowhere in that crowded room for the three of us to sit. Betsy touched me, I recall, as if to say how proud she was. The Portland High School band had come to play patriotic songs. The judge looked grave, as if to impress upon us the solemnity of the moment and the responsibilities that would come with our new rights. As I looked around he room I thought how different we all were. We had come from every corner of the earth. The color of our skin ranged from black to white, with every shade between. Twenty, thirty different languages might have been spoken in that room, and none of them but English comprehensible to me. We were young, and old. Our schooling doubtless reached from elementary to PhD's.

And yet we shared much, too, which one born here cannot know: the idea of America as someplace to be reached; a knowledge of the hardships faced in getting here; a feeling that the goal is worth the sacrifice in reaching it. And when at last the time came to recite the oath we all had memorized—renouncing foreign princes; promising to bear arms in defense of the Constitution—we did so without irony or cynicism or a grudging sense of obligation.

That's the thing about citizenship for those of us who come from someplace else. To get it, you must want it.

For myself I know that the bright blue sky of that October day, the recitation of that solemn oath, and the joy which filled that room made me know that anything was possible, and that in fulfilling the dream of a lifetime I could celebrate a new beginning.

For as long as I can remember I have recalled at such important moments the story that Uncle Diffrey told me so many years ago: the story that every Kom boy learns by heart, of the python who arrived to lead our people from want to happiness. There lies before each of us a trail, at times straight and obvious, at other times leading us up mountainsides and through thickets that obscure our futures. We follow the path, trusting in the value of hard work and perseverance to keep it in our view, and knowing that if we should not stray too far it will lead us to the place where we have always wished to be.

EPILOGUE

With friends of mine from church I once traveled by canoe down a portion of a lovely river, the Moose, whose waters run from the mountains of western Maine into the sea that separates my new home from my old. At that time I had never set foot in a canoe before, nor seen firsthand the great wilderness of which I'd so long heard reports. They are beautiful, those woods. The water of the river is clear in a way that no water in Cameroon ever is. The wildlife—swimming, flying, rustling the undergrowth on shore—is abundant. The sky is small where the river is narrow; large where it is wide. It hadn't occurred to me how used I was to the sounds of the city—of the machines, the humming currents of electricity, the shouts, the music playing in the coffeehouses, the television that runs in every doctor's office. Not just the wilderness but the stunning calm was a revelation to me. I found in the experience a part of myself that I had never known—deep, strong, wondering, silent; troubling a little, even, for its smallness in the face of the great world that had opened up to me.

Once when I came around a bend on a placid section of the river, I saw a moose. It was a large male, with an enormous set of antlers, standing at the river's edge not twenty feet away, eating of the vegetation there. Water dripped from the moose's lips as it raised its head to look. I was close enough to gaze into its clear brown eyes and to see a kind of recognition: as I acknowledged another living thing, unfrightened by its presence, so the moose acknowledged me. They are shy creatures, moose. In a moment he turned slowly, stepped from the water's edge, and disappeared. There was a kind of grace, I thought, in his ungainly gait—a grace which, indeed, I could not help envying.

Thoreau once called the Maine woods "a specimen of what God saw fit to make this world." And so they are, a place where one might be filled with something large, important, essential in the way of things that one never knew one needed until he was in possession of them.

In the five years since I became a citizen of the United States, time has run something like the river, rushing over shoals so fast as to have made me dizzy from the experience, meandering around bends, carrying me to places that I had not known I needed and now cannot imagine ever having lived without.

The greatest thing in my life is a daughter who was born to me by a woman whom I married many years after my divorce from Caroline. The time I spent with this woman was brief and difficult. I can't think of those years except bitterly, shaking my head at the ill winds of fortune that seem to follow me even as a bright future always lies ahead. Still, though, like most parents in this world who have been unlucky in their mates, I would do it all again for the promise of this child.

She herself—her spirit, her energy, her laughter, her curiosity—is the largest thing that I have ever known. Like the nature of Thoreau a child is one of those rare things that make one know for certain that God exists. She was born in Cameroon, an ocean away from me, and even so I still remember how, at the moment of her birth, I was filled as every mother, every father is when their first child arrives, with the most essential knowledge of the world.

I named my daughter Alexis Kouh-Fien Afuma. The Fien is for my grandmother; the Kouh is for my mother, who was so ecstatic to hear that the first child of her oldest son would soon be making its appearance that she leapt up from her chair to dance a jig, clapping her hands and shouting and shedding tears of joy.

As I've said, my mother loves the spotlight at such happy moments.

It meant a lot to her for her first son to bring a child into the world. In the culture of my homeland marriage is considered a divine institution, God-given and essential for the completion of a human being. There are some things one can't do—serve as a deacon in the church, for example—without having married first. One is considered irresponsible who reaches middle age without having married and parented a child.

My mother thought that Alexis looked just as I did at my birth, with the same broad nose, the same smile, the same thick head of hair. At my insistence a photographer was dispatched to Timothy's house to take photographs of my daughter—by then three months old—so that her father could begin to know her face. I cried when I looked at them for the sense they gave me that she was real at last.

I wouldn't see Alexis for eight months, and in that time could hardly stand the wait. In anticipation of her arrival I bought a new and safer car. I got a new apartment. At Country Farm I was given a discount on new furniture with which to fill the place. My friends at church chipped in to buy a crib. One day I went down to the local branch of my bank and for my daughter opened a Next-Gen savings account.

And then I waited for her to arrive.

"When am I going to see her?" I asked myself each day. It became a kind of mantra. "When am I going to see her? When am I going to see her? When am I going to see her?"

At last, nine months following her birth, she arrived on the soil of my adopted home. I suppose that I was observing her through the cloud of proud new fatherhood, but it seemed to me that my daughter greeted me with an attitude of comfortable familiarity— as if she'd known me all her life and had been only waiting for me to pick her up. She looked into my eyes without the least fear and when I smiled she smiled back at me.

Since that day I have known the joys that can only come of parenting. I have watched her grow. I've watched her learn to walk. She is a vital, curious soul—a tornado of energy, bright, happy, quick to learn. I watch in awe as she mimics every move I make. With Alexis I have learned to see with fresh eyes all those things that I had begun to be taken for granted. When I type on the computer keyboard she wants to type as well, banging her little hands upon the keys as if she has some wonderful story to tell and only wanted this novel medium in order to express herself. She pushes shopping carts. She likes to drive the car. Cameras, DVD players, remote controls are her familiars, the escalator her favorite means of rising from this earth. At the library during story-hour she refuses to stay still; at McDonald's she eats her nuggets with aplomb and runs to the PlayStation for her leisure time.

I love her more than anything on earth. With her I have at last the legacy which we Kom must bring into the world to preserve our culture and our history. She gives me strength. Her presence makes the world understandable to me. Though for the time being we must live apart, I see her face each morning when I wake and every night when I close my eyes in sleep.

I want my daughter to know the stories of her grandmother, her uncle and her cousins. I want her to know the story of her people, the Kom, and of the python whose path she too will follow, and her children after her and so on through the generations. I want her to know of the waving stalks of corn and the ripe melons and the avocados that hang in such abundance from the trees; of fufu corn and njamma-njamma; of hand-turned corn grinders and hands made as rough and hard as eucalyptus bark from the tilling of the fields. I want her to know those things. I want her to know that I love her and will never cease to love her for as long as I remain on earth.

AFTERWORD

Cameroon Defined

Cameroon is an ethnic oligarchy dominated by the country's second malignant dictator, Paul Bartholomew Biya, and members of his Bethi ethnic group. Located in the armpit of tropical Africa, and slightly larger than California, Cameroon is one of only two bilingual countries in the world with French and English as official languages, although all official documents are printed in French. There are squabbles between Francophone (an 80-percent majority speak French) and Anglophone (the remaining 20 percent speak English) regarding the exact geographical location of Cameroon, and the words "Francophone" and "Anglophone" are used derogatorily. Many Central African countries are French speaking and West African countries are English speaking. Thus, from an Anglophone's perspective, Cameroon is located in West Africa, and in Central Africa from a Francophone's perceptive. There are flippant and widespread discriminatory practices against Anglophones in education, housing, employment, etc., in a similar way that black Americans have been discriminated against.

Biya came to power in 1982, due to a political intrigue following former president Ahmadou Ahidjo's precipitous and surprise
resignation. Biya, a southern Protestant was prime minister and
constitutional successor. Ahidjo hailed from the Muslim north.
Biya's second flamboyant wife, Chantal, about half his age, is of
Lebanese descent. His benignly healthy first wife, Irene, a devout
Catholic died suddenly in the 1990s under mysterious circumstances. It was rumored that she was murdered, with French com-
plicity, along with Cameroon-based French nuns because they
knew too much.

Biya rules by decree and appoints everybody from cabinet ministers to governors, directors of private enterprises to court clerks,
who all serve at his pleasure. Since the governors are not elected,
they do not have autonomous powers as do elected American
governors. There are more than sixty cabinet ministers with dupli-
cated portfolios. I grew up in a dictatorship and voted for Biya in
1984. I voted in a democratic and free election for the first time in
the 2008 American presidential elections. He runs unopposed and
is re-elected by a near 100 percent of the electorate. He amended
the constitution in 2011 to maintain the status quo and proclaimed
himself President for life. Fortunately, Alexis will not grow up in a
dictatorship. The country is essentially governed by the President's four trusted friends and cabinet ministers. Cameroon and
the United States maintain full diplomatic relations.

Yaounde is the Cameroon's political capital, with 2 million inhabitants. The city grinds to a halt when the president is leaving or
returning from abroad. The major road is closed to commercial
activities for hours. He is hardly seen in public at home, but is
frequently spotted in European capitals with money bulging out
his pockets—a common phenomenon among African tyrants. In
March 2015, strident government-controlled media released a
highly controversial and discourteous photograph of Biya that

showed him as commander in chief standing over the caskets of Cameroonian soldiers killed by Boko Haram terrorists supposedly paying his final respects while he and his cronies were lodging in a luxurious Geneva Intercontinental Hotel. During the week of November 15, 2012, Biya squandered millions of dollars celebrating thirty years in power, which many have coined, "thirty years of legalized corruption." He spends six out of twelve months a year in Europe. His Anglophone Prime Minister is a figurehead, in a largely ceremonial post.

There is endemic corruption at the highest level throughout the country. Biya's estimated personal worth in European banks is $200 million. The French government is responsible for African's economic plight for keeping these dictators in power. I am asymmetrically opposed to direct foreign aid to African governments. Rather, I support foreign aid to specific non-governmental organizations or a certain caliber of private citizens.

In the early 1990s, Biya succumbed to international pressure and legalized a multiple-political system but only in theory. Opposition political leaders and human rights activists continued to be intimidated or arrested and public opposition rallies banned. This is one of the most repressive regimes in the world and does not make headline news in Western media. At age 82, Biya is Africa's fourth longest serving dictator. He is secretly grooming his adopted son, Frank Biya, to succeed him, another common thread among African dictators. In the 1990s, Cameroon was ranked by German based Transparency International as the most corrupt country in the world.

In recent years, Biya has ordered the closure of churches in the cities because they make excessive noise. Arrest and lengthy jail sentences have been imposed on journalists. Cabinet ministers and directors of private enterprises, including former prime ministers have been arrested and jailed under the pretext of fighting government corruption. These are his political enemies. Peaceful public demonstrations have been banned. Members of the minority English speaking have been killed or sentenced to long jail terms for publically advocating for the reinstitution of the sovereignty of formal West Cameroon.

Cameroon is an oil exporting nation but the country lacks roads and major infrastructures, unemployment and underemployment are at all-time high. Undercover armed government security agents patrol university and college campuses. The country as a whole is hardly developing, but the minority territory is worse off. The economy suffers from hyper-inflation characterized by high prices of basic commodities.

Cameroon and Nigeria came close to an-all-out war in the 1990s over the fiercely disputed oil-rich Bakassi Peninsula. The peninsula was subsequently declared Nigeria's by the International Court, but tension between the two countries remains. Young Cameroonians, including my nephew, Ivo Chahjoh Mbandam, were killed in war skirmishes in the area; their families were never notified and their remains never returned or properly buried. We don't know precisely what happened to Ivo, but he is presumed killed. He last visited his family in Bamenda in 1998. His late father visited the area to investigate but was impeded by lack of collaboration and transparency.

There is overwhelming fear on Cameroonian and African streets of the serious threats posed by Boko Haram, the central African terrorist group similar to Islamic extremists from the Middle East; the spread of the Ebola virus, as well as hunger and oppressive poverty. With more than 400 million consumers in Sub-Saharan Africa, the United States should play a more robust role in promoting market democracies. It is in the best political, economic, and security interest of the United States, as Communist China has begun to take advantage of the political vacuum in the region.

ACKNOWLEDGMENTS

It's difficult in any book to acknowledge all those people who have helped to shape its contents. Still, one has to try.

In addition to my mother, I owe the most profound debts of gratitude to my late father, Barnabas Afuma, and to the late Bobe David M. Cheng and the late Pa Andrew Ndonyi; to Doug and the Sholl family and the Scarborough Free Baptist Church who have supported me in every way imaginable; and, finally, to my brother, Timothy Tim Afuma, and his family, for taking the heat for me when everything else failed. I'd like to thank Timothy, too, and another of my brothers, Benjamin Waindim, for the countless family interviews they conducted on my behalf as I tried to understand the complex structure of our family.

I thank God for giving me the wisdom, strength, and courage to live on both sides of a dream. I thank all the members of the Afo-A-Kom Yahoo news group for their thoughtful and insightful contributions to my understanding of the culture, traditions, and family dynamics of the Kom people. I'd like to thank as well my biological father, who, though I never met him, gave me no less a start on life than my mother did. Finally, I would like to thank Thatcher Freund, whose perseverance helped to make possible the telling of my story as I have always imagined it.

We all have paths to follow that lead us to our destinies. No matter how straight or twisting these paths might be, the effort we give in walking them and discoveries we make along the way help us better understand ourselves. We couldn't take a step, though, without the other people in our lives who have held out their hands and helped to show the way to us. Even more than for their help with my book, then, I'd like to thank not just those I've named above, but everyone, both in Africa and in America, who has helped me down my Python Trail.

CPSIA information can be obtained at www.ICGtesting.com
Printed in the USA
BVOW05s1658260415

397674BV00002B/4/P